T0086383

THE VOICE OF BETTY BOOP, MAE QUESTEL

THE VOICE OF BETTY BOOP, MAE QUESTEL

JAMES D. TAYLOR, JR.

Algora Publishing
New York

Library of Congress Cataloging-in-Publication Data —

Names: Taylor, James D., 1958- author.
Title: The voice of Betty Boop, Mae Questel / James D. Taylor, Jr.
Description: New York: Algora Publishing, [2016] | Includes bibliographical
    references.
Identifiers: LCCN 2016039290 (print) | LCCN 2016042356 (ebook) | ISBN
    9781628942408 (soft cover: alk. paper) | ISBN 9781628942415 (hard cover:
    alk. paper) | ISBN 9781628942422 (pdf)
Subjects: LCSH: Questel, Mae, 1910-1998. | Voice actors and actresses—
United
    States—Biography. | Animated films—United States. | Animated television
    programs—United States.
Classification: LCC PN2287.Q5125 T39 2016 (print) | LCC PN2287.Q5125
(ebook)
    | DDC 791.4302/8092 [B] —dc23
LC record available at https://lccn.loc.gov/2016039290

Printed in the United States

So long as men can breathe, or eyes can see,
So long lives this, and this gives life to thee.
—William Shakespeare, Sonnet 18

TABLE OF CONTENTS

INTRODUCTION

Betty Boop is an iconic figure that has endured for generations and continues to amuse audiences young and old. Recognized from classic cartoons, she can be found lending her image to almost everything from automotive and motorcycle merchandise to household items and clothing. Just about anything you can think of, her sexy little figure can be seen on it. But few people know the voice that helped make her into the icon she is.

Mae Questel was an American actress and vocal artist who put the "boop" in the "boop boop a doop." Please let me make it clear, Mae Questel is not credited for originating the term "boop boop a doop" that is synonymous with Betty Boop, that honor falls to Helen Schroeder-Kane. But, it was because of Mae Questel that Betty Boop has a characteristic voice heard and remembered by millions.

This book provides a look into the life of this wonderful woman and the contributions she made. She was dedicated to her work and remained active until the last ten years of her long life. It amazed me that she found time once in a while to take a vacation, though only a few with most taken were also while working.

With four biographies "under my belt," I assumed that I had acquired the necessary tools to undertake such a project, but I realized that I had much to learn about writing about someone in modern times. For example, as much as I would like to have shared photographs and reprints of some of her later movie performances, the costs were prohibitive. Asked about reprinting the media cover of one of her recent movie appearances, the studio that produced it quoted $9,000 for a 1-inch-by-2-inch picture. The average quote for the remainder of her movie appearances ranged from $3,000 to $6,000 to reprint a 1-inch-by-2-inch picture of the media cover. One of the larger newspapers quoted $900 to reprint twenty words from a recent article. A couple of well-known actors quoted up to $500 per hour for a telephone interview. I am grateful to individuals including Woody Allen, Lou Hirsch, Doris Roberts and Bob Newhart, who shared their accounts of Mae Questel with me.

As the book came close to finish, I allowed a few close colleagues to review it. Their first question was, "What, no dirt?" Simple answer: there was none. Mae was a hardworking Jewish woman who was passionate about what she did. She had no drug and or alcohol addictions with endless rehab sessions, wild parties, arrest records, fiery divorces (well, maybe not this one), extramarital affairs, animal sacrifices, or wild religious beliefs involving "the mothership" or anything that we have grown so accustomed to nowadays that fuel the popularity of tabloids and/or many books on celebrities. "Mae made a lot of money; share that?" No. It's none of anyone's business. Yes, she was well paid, and I do have some figures, but I feel that they are not relevant to a biography about her. "Have you covered everything?" No. I'm not sure it is possible to do so. The only reliable source passed away in 1998. But, I can say that this is the most comprehensive biography about her.

I have interacted with some wonderful people while accumulating information, and I admit that I had listened to hundreds of hours of old audio recordings and viewed many hours of film to accumulate some material for this biography. With every hour I grew to honor this admirable and talented woman who entertained millions of people (and will for generations to come). I truly hope this biography expresses the honor Mae Questel should have.

Acknowledgments

As with any project of this nature, there are those who have contributed to and assisted with providing material, and at the very least, it is here that I can say thank you:

Fleischer Studios, Bronx County Historical Society, Janet W. McKee of the Recorded Sound Research Center at the Library of Congress, The Copyright Office of The Library of Congress, The New York Public Library for the Performing Arts, Billy Rose Theatre Division, Webster Theatre Guild, Office of the Registrar at Columbia University, The Indianapolis Public Library, Shore Club South Beach Hotel, University of Michigan School of Law, ASIFA-Hollywood, The Theatre Guild, University at Albany, University of Michigan School of Music and Theatre. New York County Lawyers' Association.

CHAPTER 1. 1908–1933

Mae Kwestel (later changed to Questel) was born on September 13, 1908, to Simon and Frieda Kwestel, who lived in the Bronx, New York. Birth records indicate that both parents were born in Russia and claimed Russian Jewish heritage.

The Bronx was first settled in the 1840s and is separated from Manhattan Island by the Harlem River and is itself divided by the Bronx River. From 1890 to 1900 the population rose from 88,908 to 200,507, and then to approximately 271,630 at the time of Mae's birth.

After 1890, the Bronx became a haven for tens of thousands of second-generation immigrants seeking to leave the crowded tenements of East Harlem and the Lower East side. Between 1880 and 1930, the Bronx has often been described as one of the fastest-growing urban areas of the world and because of its stable ethnic neighborhoods and housing units, it was often seen as the epitome of the latest in modern urban living. By 1910, the Russian Jewish population for the borough of the Bronx was 5.7 percent, and by 1920, that number increased to 18.2 percent. These housing units often included elevators, liveried doorman, and sunken living rooms. This resulted in the Bronx having the most multifamily dwellings and the fewest owner-occupied homes of any city or county in America, and this allowed for an intense street life, which eventually accounted for much of its nostalgia.

Mae Kwestel was born into a wonderful period of American history, a period of "transition in progress." It is considered the first decade of materialism and consumerism. The industrial age was in full swing, and mass production made prices fall to all-time lows. The electrical grid grew, increasing productivity with electric motors and lighting that allowed workers to work longer. The Sears and Roebuck and Montgomery Ward catalogs were read more than any other book besides the Bible. Teddy bears became a fad because of the 1902 cartoon depicting Teddy Roosevelt as the bear; they were mass-produced soon after.

This period also marked the flight of the Wright Brothers at Kitty Hawk; Cadillac Motor Car Company was founded: and the Indian and Harley-Davidson motorcycles were created. Henry Ford provided the first affordable car also during this period. The Ford Model T appeared on the market the year Mae was born, and the Federal Bureau of Investigation was also established.

The fashion at the turn of the century was formal and romantic; men wore long, slim trousers with a bit of fullness at the top, and the lightweight cotton-knit shirt became popular for beach and sportswear. Women wore the high, straight-front corset with long hips, making their waists as small as possible, and garters came into fashion during this era. The skirt lengths became shorter to allow for stepping into the new automobile and trolley easier, and a cap with goggles and a linen duster made up the motoring outfit. The high-button shoe lasted into this era as well. People were very clothes conscious and often described as "costumy," with these styles leading into the 1920s.

This was the industrial age, and during this period, industrial growth encouraged trades people to practice their arts. Their businesses grew as demand for their services grew. Records show that Simon Kwestel owned and operated a fairly successful embroidery business at 1833 Washington Avenue in the Bronx, about fifteen minutes from the family home. Records also show that as of 1912, Mr. Kwestel employed four men, twelve women, and three children between fourteen and sixteen years of age, and the following year, seven men and ten women were employed. In 1915, the address 1178 Longwood Avenue, which about ten minutes from the Washington Avenue address, is mentioned, and a capital base of $3,000 was declared. That address and the figures remain steady until 1920. Several addresses appear to be recorded in various city registers, but the Longwood address appears more often than the others. In 1918, Simon registered for the draft of World War I, and the address of the business was 1180 Longwood Avenue; perhaps the business expanded.

As the growth of industry brought in immigrants, more people were exposed to different cultures, and these activities were frequent. Fred and Adele Astaire made their Broadway debut; "Yip! Yip! Yaphank" by Irving Berlin opened on Broadway, and Gilda Gray inspired a dance craze after she performed "the shimmy" in a Broadway show. Mae's parents would have, at some point, exposed their children to the rich cultural events happening in New York at the time. Early accounts mention that Mae showed a precocious ability to recite at the age of two and a half, and she gave public performances in elementary school and at charity events at the age of five. An account of her childhood mentions that as a child she "pleased and taunted her playmates with her ability to 'ape.'" About this time, Mae had fallen down a flight of stairs, which gave her a scar on her right cheek that was hardly perceptible. Mae later shared that she was "Little Miss Mimic at five because my mother was a frustrated singer and dialectician." A few condensed biographies mention that her parents were very against the idea of her performing, but her statement about her mother gives rare insight into her childhood, and there is an excellent chance that her parents supported her.

By 1916, she had performed at Carnegie Hall and Town Hall. What a wonderful time to influence a young girl like Mae Questel. Mae would have most certainly attended the New York

World's Fair (or more precisely, the Bronx International Exposition of Science, Arts and Industries) that opened in June 1918 in commemoration of the three-hundredth anniversary of the settlement of the borough of the Bronx. The grounds included twenty-five acres near the Bronx River and subway stations. Most prominent were an enormous swimming pool with faux rock features, a nearby roller coaster, and many Coney Island–like rides and games. One of the most popular attractions was the submarine *Holland*, the first submarine commissioned by the United States Navy. The sights and sounds that a young girl such as Mae would have experienced must have been slightly overwhelming and fabulous.

Mae also would have seen such shows as Madame Torelli's Comedy Circus, various vaudeville acts, bands, and open-air performances. Such an experience would have had a profound effect on a young girl, and soon after, Mae began to perform at school, charitable, and community functions.

Perhaps the earliest credit mentioning Mae's performance is in David Belasco's *Daddies*, which played at the Belasco Theatre on 44th Street in New York. It opened on August 5, 1918, and ran through an unknown closing date; it then was performed at the Lyceum Theater on 45th Street in New York. *Daddies* is about a number of hard-boiled American bachelors, old college mates, and men of big affairs, who, at an annual reunion, vote to adopt a group of foreign-war orphans. Mae was only about ten at the time; her name is not mentioned in the playbill or at least on opening night at the Belasco Theater, but an article written by Ada Patterson in *Theatre Magazine* published in January 1918 may shed some light:

> *Daddies* might fittingly have been called 'Babies' or 'Adoptions'. Lorna Volare, leading a quintet of children under the age of eight years of age, captivates the hearts and stimulates the imagination of the audiences of every age that flocks to the Belasco Theatre. [*Theatre Magazine*, January 1918. pp 350–351]

Following the article is a photograph of David Belasco sitting in front of what appears to be five little girls; he's telling them a story. The only name given for any of the children is Lorna Volare, who is the child on the far left. It is very possible that Mae is one of the remaining children. If I had to guess, I believe she is the middle child.

Around 1922, Mae began her studies at Morris High School on Boston Road at East 166th Street in the Bronx. Morris was the first public high school in the Bronx. Hoping to learn more about her time at high school, I contacted Morris Educational Campus (as it is now called), and my contact indicated that transcripts are no longer available that far back. In 2002, as part of an overall restructuring and downsizing of New York City's high schools, Morris was closed. The building was renamed the Morris Campus and now houses small specialty schools. The only surviving bit of information about Mae's time at Morris is that she had received a medal in her Spanish class. Notable alumni of Morris High School include Milton Berle and Herman Muller, who won a Nobel Prize in medicine. Mae would have graduated about 1926.

Based on early information, Mae attended the newly founded Theatre Guild School in 1923 while she was still attending high school. During her short time there, her teacher Joseph G. Geiger changed her name to Questel, which Mae said in a 1989 interview "was okay by me. You know he gave Sylvia Sidney her start too." While at the Theatre Guild, she studied dancing, singing and dramatics. But her traditional Jewish Orthodox grandparents strongly opposed her perusing a career in show business, and Mae was forced to quit. This did not dissuade her, and just after graduating high school between 1927 and 1928, she taught elocution at her parents' house.

I encountered several short biographies about Mae that indicate that she had attended Columbia University. The Registrar Services Associate of the Office of the Registrar of Columbia University informed me that her name does not appear in records of the period. Other variations of her name, including Kwestel, did not show up in its records, either.

Despite the verbal objections she received from her grandparents, Mae was hooked on show business and entered an impersonation contest. On December 31, 1929, the *New York Morning Telegraph* announced that Mae Questel had won both the "boop-boop-a-doop" contest and the Helen Kane cash prize for the best imitation of her individual style of singing a song. Mae won $100 in gold from Helen Kane and four additional days' booking at the RKO (Radio Keith Orpheum) Theater.

The phrase "boop-boop-a-doop," or some close variation of it, is, for the most part, meaningless and branches out of phrases used in vocal music that grew out of a jazz style called "scat," where a performer often improvises words as if he or she were another musical instrument. One of the great scat singers of the period was Cab Calloway, and in 1931 he recorded a song "The Scat Song" that included the following line: "When your sweetie tells you, everything'll be okay, Just skeep-beep de bop-bop beep bop bo-dope skeetle-at-de-op-de-day!" Other notable scat singers include Dizzy Gillespie, Bing Crosby, Louis Armstrong, and Sammy Davis Jr., just to name a few.

Mae played other RKO theaters after the contest, mainly in vaudeville shows, for about ten additional weeks. Because of these paid performances, she could now regard herself as a professional actress. At that time, Mae was living at 1165 Andersen Avenue in the Bronx, New York, and three days prior to the date of the news article she had substituted for Helen, who was sick, at RKO Proctor's 58th Street Theatre, located at 154 East 58th Street, an approximately seventeen-minute trip from Mae's home. The theater was located a few blocks from Central Park.

The theater first opened on December 20, 1929, on the same site as Proctor's Pleasure Palace Palm Gardens, which opened in 1895. RKO Proctor's 58th Street Theatre was described as spectacular, with a high-vaulted grand foyer, ornate staircases, and a 3,163-seat Spanish Renaissance auditorium with a "midnight sky" ceiling that most certainly was a showpiece. In 1929, F. F. Proctor chose to retire and sold all his theaters to the RKO circuit, and it maintained the name for several decades.

Helen Kane

There is probably no better time to introduce Helen Kane and give a short biography about her. Helen played an important role in Mae Questel's life during the 1930s. Helen Kane was born Helen Claire Schroeder on August 4, 1903, in the Bronx, New York, to a German father, who held many different jobs, and an Irish mother, who worked as a housekeeper. It appears that Helen was influenced by the stage at an early age; and while she was attending the St. Anselin's Parochial School, she convinced her mother to spend three dollars for a costume so she could dress as a queen in her first theatrical role.

By 1918, Helen was on stage professionally touring the Orpheum Circuit. She spent the early 1920s trouping in vaudeville as a singer and a kick line dancer with a theater engagement "All Jazz Revue," and she soon after played the New York Palace for the first time in 1921. Helen later reminisced: "I was on with Clayton, Jackson, Durante, Bill Robinson, Ken Murray, Lulu McConnell and Ruth Etting. When you came in here you had to be tops. There was a great deal of talent."

In 1920, Helen began touring with the Marx Brothers and later shared a story that Chico saw Helen sitting in an agent's office. She said she had "sneaked away from school to be an actress" and mentioned that her mother would have killed her had she known. Helen played the role as ingénue and served as nursemaid for Groucho's and Chico's babies. Helen recounted that she changed their diapers and wheeled their carriages in every city in the United States, she but valued the time she spent with the Marx Brothers, who taught her a great deal.

Helen Kane joined in the Marx Brothers production of *On the Balcony* when it went to London in 1922 and opened at the Coliseum, St. Martin's Lane; she performed the role of Dorothy Gould.

In 1924, Helen married department store buyer Joseph Kane and took his name professionally. The following year Helen starred in a *Night in Spain*, which ran for 174 performances at the 44th Street Theater in New York. She earned $150 a week under the direction of J. J. you're. Helen later recalled that while singing a popular song of the time, "That's My Weakness Now," she interpolated the lyrics "boop-boop-a-doop" in rehearsal. It was an instant hit and soon after, her name was up in lights, and it seemed that her life had changed almost overnight. "One day I had fifty cents and next day I had $50,000," she said in an interview several years later. Helen's agent secured the amount of $5,500 a week for her to perform in Oscar Hammerstein's production *Good Boy*, where she introduced her hit "I Wanna Be Loved by You." She told a reporter in 1928, "Money was falling off trees. I got $5000.00 at one of those big society parties just to sing four or five choruses of *Button up Your Overcoat*."

By mid-1928, Helen had recorded many records and was regarded as a full-fledged fad with the appearance of Helen Kane dolls, look-a-like contests, and appearances on radio and in nightclubs. She was something fresh and interesting, often regarded as a Kewpie doll look-a-like with her round face and large brown eyes, with a voice like a baby squeak with a Bronx accent. By 1929, Paramount signed Helen to make a series of musicals, and her popularity made her in great demand. There was mention that she was experiencing high levels of stress because of a hectic schedule, and some effects were noticed. It has been suggested that Helen's illness had prevented her from appearing at Proctor's 58th Street Theater and was a result of this stress.

What was Helen's loss was most certainly Mae's gain; it launched Mae Questel's career. It was also at about this time that Mae had married Leo Balkin. It is not clear how they met, but he was from Queens. Surviving records show that he was a textile importer, had completed at least two years of college, and was about a year older than Mae.

In early April 1929, Max Fleischer changed the name of the studio from Out of the Inkwell, Inc., founded in 1921, to Fleischer Studios, the same name that the studio uses to date. The studio quickly began to produce what it could afford—*Song Car-Tunes*. The success Max had with the popular Koko the Clown and the bouncing ball cartoons gave him the confidence to approach Paramount Pictures, and he soon concluded a deal that included Paramount financing and distributing all of Fleischer Studios productions. By the end of 1929, Fleischer Studios was located at 1600 Broadway, New York.

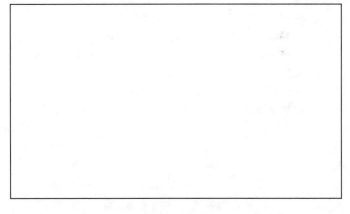

The bouncing ball (seen in the picture of the Boswell Sisters singing in the *Sleepy Time Down South* short from 1932, the ball is just above the word *Sleep-y*) is a device used in video recording to visually indicate the rhythm of a song or melody. Invented by Fleischer Studios, it was first used in 1925 for the *Song Cartoon*

series of animated cartoons. In those early films, the bouncing ball was not animated, but by capturing a luminescent ball on the end of a stick being bounced across the screen by someone from the studio on film, the stick was rendered invisible. The ball would often appear as white on black.

Although other cartoon producers already had sound tracks, none actually "talked," and Max soon made a decision to produce cartoons that actually talked. His new series would be called "Talkartoons." Paramount showed their enthusiasm with the idea and published "Paramount Talkartoons are something entirely new and entirely different from anything ever seen and heard before. For the first time, cartoons will be actually talking pictures."

Paramount was enthused with his idea, and Max Fleischer and Fleischer Studios changed the name of the highly successful *Song Car-Tunes* to *Screen Songs*. The musical bouncing ball cartoon became an "astounding, wildly successful runaway hit."

A fresh new figure appeared at about the same time on the silver screen that pushed Fleischer Studios' popular Koko the Clown off center stage—a Walt Disney character called Mickey Mouse. Max quickly responded to this new character from his rival Disney Studios by replacing Koko's dog, Fritz, with another canine who was a much "tougher, cigar-chewing, somewhat lecherous, piano-playing jazz hound" named Bimbo, named after a dog owned by Max's son Richard Fleischer.

Bimbo was designed to give Mickey Mouse "a run for his money," with a personality that was a complete opposite of Mickey. By the time the sixth Talkartoon *Dizzy Dishes* (which first aired on August 9, 1930) went into production, it was clear that Bimbo was not keeping up with the mouse's popularity and Max realized that something was missing—a love interest.

But, while Disney was enjoying the popularity of its new character and Fleischer Studios was trying to make its way into the now-popular animation world, it had to overcome the somber and even tragic atmosphere of the stock market crash in October 1929. "Black Tuesday" certainly did not put audiences in the mood for watching a cartoon. Max Fleischer had to develop a character that would go above and beyond, and Fleischer Studios was up to the challenge. His answer was and still is his greatest character of all: Betty Boop.

Fleischer Studios felt that *Dizzy Dishes* required a female character who would act as an entertainer and who would work well with Bimbo's personality. At first, as can be seen in the short *Dizzy Dishes*, the character Fleischer Studios came up with was half-dog and half-human with a very clunky appearance, with a large head and even larger behind, but it did have round, saucerlike eyes and shapely feminine legs. There seems to be, and will continue to be, debate over Mae's very early voice contributions to the Betty Boop cartoons. It is believed that she provided voices in three of the cartoons in 1930 including *Dizzy Dishes*, but Margie Hines is also given credit. Most who have looked into the matter do agree (and I believe they are right) that Mae's first voice work was in *Silly Scandals*, released on May 23, 1931.

Paramount was enthusiastic about the new character and requested more. Over the span of the next few cartoons, Fleischer Studios refined the character, and the doglike features did not last long. The rather gross-looking character morphed into one that was sexier, with a tiny waist above long, shapely legs and a "very human bosom." Now the search was on for the perfect voice. Many "squeaky female" voices were tried, but none seemed to fit Max Fleischer's idea of the perfect voice. Max was seeking a voice for Betty Boop that was not only squeaky but could sound cute and sexy, be able to sing, and, above all, to say and sing "boop-boop-a-doop" in a certain way.

Word of Mae Questel's unique talents quickly spread because of the Kane contest, and Mae moved from this performance to what seems to be her first appearance on film. In 1930 Mae joined with famed Major League Baseball pitcher Waite Hoyt, who played with the New York Yankees. In addition to being a mortician in the off-season, Mr. Hoyt was also a singer and teamed with veteran songwriter J. Fred Coots in a nine-minute Vitaphone short film *A Battery of Songs*, released on May 9, 1930.

Mae Questel's popularity increased with each program on the radio in which she performed impersonations and mimicked celebrities. An account of one such program was when Mae performed an impersonation of Marlene Dietrich. Mae stood in front of the microphone and went through a variety of gestures and facial movements, throwing her arms about, a favorite habit of hers she informed an interviewer at the time. "Sometimes I find myself making a face at the mike. I don't know why, because somehow I feel that the little black box is my friend," Mae said. Mae made additional appearances during the same year at Namm's department store in Brooklyn, Gimbel's in Philadelphia, and Stern Brothers in New York, where she sang songs, recited a little kitty poem, and impersonated several famous people such as Maurice Chevalier and Irene Bordoni. These appearances caught the attention of the person who would launch Mae Questel into a career that would be remembered forever.

Richard Fleischer mentions in his book *Out of the Inkwell* that his dad found the perfect voice for Betty Boop with Mae Questel in 1931, and furthermore indicated that her voice and Betty Boop quickly became synonymous, and that Mae even looked like Betty Boop. Mae reviewed hundreds of reels to help her with finding the voice that Max was looking for. Mae stayed with the series until it ended 118 pictures later. This number also corresponds with the number of pictures Mae quoted in an interview in the 1980s and a number given during *Kane v. Fleischer*. Appendix 2 includes a list of all the Betty Boop cartoons that Mae voiced. Mae performed other voices in the Betty Boop cartoons, and in Appendix 2, I attempt to give an accurate list of all her contributions to the Betty Boop cartoons. The list certainly shows Mae's diversity and talent, meeting a wide range of voice demands. Unfortunately, if Fleischer Studios maintained any information or records of who voiced which characters and how many they voiced of those characters, they were destroyed in 1943. Twelve years of corporate records, statements, tax reports, production records, film delivery records, laboratory, payroll, and social security records for more than seven hundred employees were destroyed—on purpose.

By Betty Boop's ninth picture, *Minding the Baby*, which first aired on November 26, 1931, the character looked completely human, and it was in that cartoon that she was finally named Betty Boop. Also the Talktoon series was renamed the Betty Boop series.

It appears that Fleischer Studios had another hit on its hands, and Paramount was, of course, thrilled because merchandising also took off (which most certainly included appearances by Mae Questel). This included Betty Boop dolls and clothes, and the list is rather long. Furthermore, Max incorporated top name jazz performers such as Cab Calloway and Louis Armstrong, among other entertainers, including Ethel Merman and Rudy Vallee, in the Betty Boop cartoons.

To give an idea of what it took to produce a cartoon, it took approximately one-hundred artists working full-time for five weeks to produce one cartoon short of, on the average, about 6 minutes. Then an orchestra was used for the synchronization of sounds, voices, and singing through the use of a metronome. It took Fleischer about a year to complete his first six-minute cartoon consisting of twelve thousand separate drawings traced over onto celluloid and then photographed by a still camera for film.

Max Fleischer patented several unique devices that were groundbreaking for the cartoon industry. Perhaps the best known was the rotoscope that he applied for a patent on December 6, 1915. To prove that the rotoscope worked, he had to shoot some footage, and Fleischer Studios believes it was of Boy Scouts working with semaphore flags and that the film may have been lost or damaged. Max received the patent in 1917.

Rotoscoping is an animation technique in which animators trace over footage, frame by frame, for use in live-action and animated films. In the visual effects industry, the term rotoscoping refers to the technique of manually creating a matte for an element on a live-action plate so it may be composited over another background. Max used rotoscoping in several cartoons, most notably the Cab Calloway dance routines in three Betty Boop cartoons. Mae would often spend many hours in front of a microphone watching the film roll and listening to a metronome click to get her voice timing just right over the span of many days just for one cartoon short.

Mae later shared an account of the production of the Betty Boop cartoons. "When we first started, there was a bouncing ball right there on the side of the cartoon and we'd follow the ball with our words or lyrics. It took a week to make one cartoon and we had to rehearse for three days." Mae continued, explaining that as the cartoon progressed over the years, the voice-over was done first, and "animation was added to fit." This new process allowed her to perform voice characterization in as many as ten cartoons and helped with the increase in productions.

This rise in popularity was enhanced with a new means— television—and Betty Boop became the first animated character broadcast via this new form. The *New York Times* reported on September 25, 1931, in an article titled "Television Stages a Talking Picture," that at 7:45 p.m., Max Fleischer would draw some of his cartoons before the television-sending station and that visitors would see the drawings reproduced on the very large projection screen. The following is from *Gateway to Radio* by Major Ivan Firth and gives an idea of the event:

> But perhaps the most successful of all our programs was that in which Max Fleischer, the beloved creator of Koko the Clown, Barnacle Bill, Betty Boop, Bimbo, and a host of other pen and ink stars, appeared for us in person in a presentation of the first animated cartoon to be televised. Standing in front of the brilliant light, Max Fleischer, while carrying on a running conversation with Miss Erskine, drew with rapid sure strokes of his charcoal pencil the pert Miss known to millions as Betty Boop. Suddenly, lo and behold, Miss Boop (Betty to her intimates) came to life, rolled her eyes, blinked her famous lashes, and then, without more ado opened her pouting mouth and sang her Boop-a-doop song, with all the allure of lowered lids. So successful was this feature

that it was selected as the only program to be presented at the World's Radio Fair at Madison Square Garden on the ten foot screen. [Firth, Major Ivan, *The Gateway to Radio*, pg. 305–306]

Although scheduled for only one performance, the program was repeated nearly thirty times. This, of course, delighted Mr. Wells, who was the special announcer. Although Mae was providing voicing for Betty Boop as early as May 1931, whether she provided voicing for that performance is not clear.

Although Betty Boop, for the most part, remained on the silver screen, certainly no one could have anticipated the quick popularity of the character, and it was clear that Fleischer Studios and Paramount were very pleased—to say the very least. Betty Boop's rise to fame even surpassed a certain mouse's, and more was to follow.

Not only was Mae Questel busy with voices for the now popular Betty Boop, but she also continued with other Broadway interests, including a role in *Wayward*, an American drama that was an adaptation of Mateel Howe Farnham's novel *Wild Beauty*. *Wayward* starred Nancy Carroll and Richard Arlen, and Mae played the role of Chorine, a showgirl. The film was released by Paramount on February 19, 1932, to lukewarm reviews from film critic Mordaunt Hall: "Not precisely engrossing notwithstanding instances of competent acting. Its development is somewhat amateurish and mechanical and the characters are invariably frightfully exaggerated specimens of humanity." Even so, demands for Mae Questel's talent grew, and she continued to be busy.

Mae later shared a story about when Maurice Chevalier visited the Paramount Studios at the release of a film he starred in *One Hour with You*, released March 23, 1932. When he arrived at the studio, he wanted to meet Mae and watch a Betty Boop cartoon. She, Mr. Chevalier, and a small number of Paramount brass were ushered into the screening room, and she was given the place of honor next to Mr. Chevalier. Mae said, "Sitting in the dark, I suddenly felt his arm around my neck. I was 20 years old at the time and I was too frozen to say a word."

Following the show, when the lights came back on, Mr. Chevalier said, "That was delightful. I would like to take you to dinner." He mentioned his new picture *One Hour with You* and wanted her to see it. Mae told him that she would be delighted to go to dinner and that "he didn't need to pick me up because my husband would do that." She added that she and her husband enjoyed the show but that dinner did not happen.

I encountered a few references to Mae appearing in *One Hour with You* as an office worker, but in reviewing the movie twice, I did not see her. At 1 hour, 6 minutes into the movie there is a scene involving two women in an office situation. One woman folds a letter and then hands it to the next woman, who places it in an envelope and then stamps it. Neither woman even closely resembles Mae Questel, nor at any point in the movie do I either hear or see Mae. Her name is not mentioned in the movie credits.

During the same year, she participated in a couple of Paramount film shorts. These obscure films were very difficult to locate. The first was *Knowmore College*, an offbeat musical about a college whose students were not making the grade. The school is at risk of losing funding until Professor Vallee (Rudy Vallee) steps in to save the day and begins instructing the class by making the lesson rhyme and set it to music. Mae Questel plays a dumb coed chewing and snapping her gum in class, while Professor Vallee instructs the class of misfits. Mae's Bronx accent is clear as she recites her lessons. She is prominently featured at the end of the film with a talking skeleton.

Also released that year was *The Musical Doctor*. The setting is Dr. Vallee's (Rudy Vallee) musical hospital, where patients with music-related disorders that are, of course, treated with therapeutic melodies. Mae played Nurse Clef and is first seen sitting in front of a rather odd-looking telephone switchboard with certain elements resembling a pipe organ. Nurse Clef is chatting with Nurse Octave and then receives a call from Dr. Sharp about Miss Barcelona, who requires a dose of Spanish music. Dr. Vallee expresses himself throughout the film in song, visits a patient, and prescribes a strict regimen of music—a fox-trot, some blues, and "a salad made of light ballad"—as Nurse Clef tosses in a few "boop-boop-a-doops" from time to time.

Max Fleischer had followed the popularity of a certain one-eyed sailor with rather enormous arms in Elzie Segar's Thimble Theater daily comic strip of Popeye the Sailor. Max had a hunch that the character from the comic strip would work even better on the silver screen, and on November 17, 1932, Max signed a contract with King Features Syndicate, the owner of the rights to the character Popeye.

King Features did not share the same enthusiasm that Max Fleischer had about their character on the silver screen and requested that a test cartoon be shown in theaters before May 30, 1933. That a great deal was riding on the test cartoon was clear, and major decisions were made about how to animate a static character to the movie screen. Problems such as his voice, movement, associated characters, and even a theme song had to be decided on in a very short period. It is interesting to note that Popeye's super strength was at that point the result of rubbing the head of a magic whiffle hen. The eating of spinach, which gave Popeye his superstrength, was solely a Fleischer Studios creation. Clearly making the switch to something other than what loyal followers of the comic strip were familiar with on paper only added to the many concerns Fleischer Studios had in transforming the character to moving pictures on the silver screen.

Fleischer Studios decided that the best method of revealing its new character was not to have him appear in a cartoon by himself but to introduce him in a Betty Boop cartoon *Popeye the Sailor*, which premiered on July 14, 1933. Fleischer Studios took a chance on how to animate Popeye and gave him some rather peculiar traits, such as a galloping gait, a unique laugh, and an always visible pipe from which an occasional toot would emerge.

The first cartoon began with an opening theme song, in which Mae Questel contributed to the real-life images of newspapers exiting a printing press with "Popeye a Movie Star" on the front-page headlines. The cartoon continued with an introduction to other characters that would remain with Popeye throughout the series, such as Bluto and Olive Oyl (voiced by Mae Questel). When Bluto kidnaps Olive and when Popeye jumps on stage and joins in, a clearly topless Betty Boop (with flower ring or leis covering some of her bosom) begins dancing a hula dance. Eventually Popeye, after eating his spinach, beats up Bluto and then saves Olive Oyl from a speeding train. Mae Questel pulled double duty in this cartoon as the voice of Betty Boop and Olive Oyl.

The reaction from the Depression-era theater audience was just as everyone had hoped; the laughter and delight were clearly a green light for Fleischer Studios and Paramount to continue with the series. It was apparent soon after that Popeye's success even surpassed that of Betty Boop, who was, to that point, the only competitor for Mickey Mouse. Popeye soon became even more popular than the mouse. Mae Questel would be very busy with additional voicing, certainly a task that she took on with the same great enthusiasm for which she is so well known. But a storm cloud was looming on the horizon, and Fleischer Studios could not but notice it coming.

CHAPTER 2. 1932–1936

In May 1932, Helen Kane filed a lawsuit against Max Fleischer and Paramount Publix Corporation for $250,000 for "Deliberate Caricature" that she felt produced "unfair competition." The Lower Court of New York ruled in favor of the defendant, the case was appealed and went to the Supreme Court in 1934. As the media began to report on the "circus like" events of the trial, Mae and Leo Balkin had their first son, Robert born on August 7, 1933, in New York, New York. I believe this date to be correct, but I have been unsuccessful with communicating with that side of the family to confirm or deny it. One of the two family members (on the Questel side) who did respond to my inquiries mentioned that a cartoon of a pregnant Betty Boop was drawn by one of her animators and given to Mae while she was carrying Robert. I was unsuccessful in locating it.

As the Balkins enjoyed their blessed child, the trial continued in the Supreme Court of the State of New York, Appellate Division, and the media's portrayal of it was somewhat comical and can be read in an example of a New York Times headline: "Court Solemn as Helen Kane Boops out Grief." Another article mentions that the abundance of "boop-boop-a-doop," "whadda-dahed," and "vo-do-deo-dued" had bewildered the court stenographer and constantly required assistance with spelling. A January 18, 1933, article in *The Brooklyn Daily Eagle* mentioned that Helen Kane would be back in the limelight as she prepared for her legal battle. "I'm sore, but I think the trial will be fun."

Mae Questel and Max Fleischer

For Max Fleischer, the trial was not fun. Mae Questel was approached to give the only testimony for the defendants Max Fleischer and Fleischer Studios, as others, such as Bonnie Poe, Margy Hines, Little Ann Little (other voices used by Fleischer Studios), gave testimony for the defendant Paramount Publix

Corporation. Mae appeared on the stand on May 4, 1934. The transcript erroneously spells hername as Questal.

The first copy of the full court transcript (462 pages) that I attempted to review went missing from the stacks of the New York State Education Department; it almost killed this project until another copy was located and supplied to me by Mr. Jordan, director of library services, New York County Lawyers Association. Because of the association's generosity, I am able to share Mae Questel's testimony.

Samuel Robert Weltz served as the attorney for the plaintiff, N. William Welling served as attorney for Max Fleischer, and Austin C. Keough served as attorney for the Paramount Corporation; the Honorable Edward J. McGoldrick presided.

Mae Questal—For Defendants—Direct.
Mae Questal, 444 Central Park West, called as a witness in behalf of the Fleischer Studios, Inc., being first duly sworn, testifies as follows:

Direct exanimation by Mr. Welling.
Q. What is your occupation, Miss Questal?
A. Actress.
Q. How long have you been a professional actress?
A. About four or five years.
Q. Before that what did you do for a living?
A. I taught elocution.
Q. How long did you do that?
A. About two years.
Q. Did you participate in any Helen Kane contests?
A. I did.
Q. In what year?
A. I think 1928 or 1929.
Q. In what theatre?
A. The Fordham Theatre.
Q. Did you win a prize?
A. Yes.
Q. Was it the first prize?
A. Yes.
Q. And what was the prize?
A. Four days' booking at the theatre.
Q. Did you play that theatre for the four days?

A. I did.

Q. Did you ever see Helen Kane perform publicly before you entered this contest?

A. I did.

Q. How often?

A. About four or five times in theatres.

Q. Did you ever see her in moving pictures before you went into this contest?

A. I did.

Q. Do you know how often?

A. Well, I don't know how often, no.

Q. Did you hear any phonograph records by Helen Kane before you entered this contest?

A. No.

Q. After this engagement at the Fordham, what did you do after that?

A. I played in the R.K.O. theaters in vaudeville.

Q. In this act that you went in, at which you won the prize, what kind of an act did you put out; what did you do?

A. You mean the contest prize?

Q. Yes.

A. I just sang a song and for two days I played a single in the theatre and recited a poem.

Q. What song did you sing in this prize performance?

A. The song that won the contest, with "He's So Unusual."

Q. How long did you continue with the R.K.O.?

A. For about 10 weeks.

Q. What theatres, what sections did you cover?

A. The Metropolitan district.

Q. Will you describe your performance during those 10 weeks?

Mr. Weltz: Objected to.

(Overruled. Exception by plaintiff.)

A. I sang cute songs, I mimicked people, and that is about all.

Q. What songs did you sing?

A. I sang the song I won the contest with, "He's So Unusual"

Q. Any other songs?

A. I sang a Chevalier song, a song about a little boy who

was very naughty in school.

Q. What did you do after this 10 weeks' engagement?

A. I played the other theatres and I recorded the Betty Boop pictures, and sang on the radio.

Q. What theatres in this country have you played in?

A. Almost all of the New York theatres.

Q. Almost all of what   ?

A. The New York theatres.

Q. Yes.

A. Just recently the out-of-town theatres.

Q. Were you engaged to do the recording for the voice of Betty Boop in the Fleischer cartoons?

A. Yes.

Q. Who engaged you?

A. Mr. Diamond.

Q. Through what office did you obtain that employment or engagement?

Mr. Weltz: Objected to.

(Sustained. Exception by Mr. Welling.)

Q. Did you sing before Mr. Diamond, before he engaged you?

Mr. Weltz: Objected to as incompetent, irrelevant and immaterial.

(Overruled. Exception.)

A. Yes.

Q. What song did you sing?

Mr. Weltz: Objected to. The Court: Sustained.

Q. I think you testified that you sang on the radio?

A. Yes.

Q. Do you recall when you started that engagement?

A. I do not recall.

Q. Was it in the year 1932?

A. I think so.

Q. What was the name of the act which you performed on the radio?

A. "Mae Questal, the Mimic on the Air."

Q. After that, did you play any act on the road?

A. Yes, the past year.

Q. What was the name of that act?

A. Betty Boop.

Mr. Weltz: Are you talking about 1933?

Mr. Welling: Yes.

Q. Are you playing at the present time, Miss Questal?

A. No, I just completed an engagement.

Q. What was the name of the act?

A. Betty Boop.

Q. What?

A. Mae Betty Boop Questal.

Q. How long have you been playing this act, Miss Questal?

A. About two months.

Q. Will you describe that act?

Mr. Weltz: Objected to as incompetent, irrelevant and immaterial, and particularly I call your Honor's attention to the fact that this is all subsequent to the institution of this suit.

(Overruled. Exception by plaintiff.)

The Court: If counsel is referring to a public performance.

Q. Public performance?

A. I sing a Betty Boop number, a few Betty Boop numbers, and in the last number I do character studies of Mae West, Zazu Pitts and the Old Irish Woman, also Maurice Chevalier.

Q. Miss Questal, in these performances that you have just described, was there a placard on the stage naming the act?

A. Yes.

Q. Of course, you have not that placard with you; it belongs to the theatre?

A. Yes, sir.

Q. How is the act named on the placard?

Mr. Weltz: Objected to, unless first the date is fixed. Are you referring to the Mae Betty Boop Questal act?

Mr. Welling: Yes.

Mr. Weltz: Objected to as incompetent, irrelevant and immaterial.

(Overruled. Exception by plaintiff.)

A. It was Betty Boop on one side, and Mae Questal on the other.

Q. Will you direct your attention now back to 1931? In that year did you make any public appearances in department stores?

Mr. Weltz: Objected to as incompetent, irrelevant and immaterial, and no bearing on the issues here.

The Court: The question may be conclusive that there were public appearances.

Q. Did you make public appearances in department stores in the year 1931?

A. Yes.

Q. Do you recall in which department stores you made those public appearances?

A. Namm's, in Brooklyn.

Mr. Weltz: I object to the places where she appeared, on the same grounds as I have heretofore objected. Will your Honor give me a general objection and exception?

The Court: Yes. Objection overruled.

Q. Continue.

A. Namm's, in Brooklyn; Gimbel's, in Philadelphia, and one or two other department stores in this city. I am sorry, but I really don't remember very well.

Q. I show you this page and ask you whether this refreshes your recollection (showing witness paper)?

A. Yes.

Q. What other department stores in New York did you appear in, in public?

A. Stern Brothers.

Mr. Weltz: On what dates?

Q. On what date?

A. November 28, 1931.

Q. Did you appear in any department stores publicly in Newark?

A. Yes.

Q. Did you put on an act or demonstration publicly in those department stores?

Mr. Weltz: Objected to on the same grounds.

(Overruled. Exception by plaintiff.)

A. I did.

Q. Will you describe it as in what month and what year you appeared in these department stores publicly?

A. That I don't remember.

Q. Was it in the month of November, 1931?

A. That particular Stern Brothers, I think, was.

Q. I show you this and ask you whether this refreshes your recollection as to the date when you put on the demonstration in Stern Brothers (showing witness paper)?

A. Yes.

Q. What date was that?

A. November 28, 1931.

Q. Were the demonstrations in the other department stores that you have mentioned in the same month, or the following month?

A. I think so. I think they were around the same time.

Q. Will you describe the act or demonstration that you put on publicly in these department stores?

Mr. Weltz: Objected to.

(Overruled. Exception by plaintiff.)

A. I sang a Betty Boop song, and recited a little kitty poem.

Q. Was any public announcement made in your presence to the people who watched the demonstration as to who you were, your identity?

Mr. Weltz: Objected to. (Sustained. Exception.)

Q. What public announcement, if any, of this performance, was made to the people watching the demonstration?

Mr. Weltz Objected to.

(Sustained. Exception.)

Q. Was Max Fleischer there with you?

A. Yes, sir.

Cross-examination by Mr. Weltz.

Q. Miss Questal, you have done quite a little of mimicking during the past few years, haven't you?

A. Yes.

Q. One of the characters whom you mimicked was Maurice Chevalier?

A. Yes.

Q. Did you mimic Fanny Brice?

A. Yes.

Q. Tell me the names of the other people that you mimicked?

A. I exaggerated—I made an exaggeration of the character.

Q. When you mimicked you sang or acted in such a way

as to give the impression of the impersonation of the person to whom you referred; isn't that correct?

A. An exaggeration of the person that I referred to.

Q. You intended to identify that particular person in your mimicking?

A. Yes.

Q. When you sing in impersonation of the people whom you mimic, I presume that customarily when you sing, you sing the songs with which these particular actors or actresses are identified, isn't that so?

A. Yes.

Q. Take Maurice Chevalier, for instance; if you mimic him, would you sing the song "Hello, Beautiful"— these people know Chevalier as the man who sings "Hello, Beautiful"?

(Objected to Sustained.)

Q. When you sing in imitation of Fannie Brice, you sing or pick out the song and sing it for which she was well known; isn't that so?

A. Yes.

Q. And Fannie Brice, you sing "I am an Indian"?

A. Yes.

Q. You called yourself "Mae Betty Boop Questal"; is that correct?

A. Yes.

Q. And the Betty Boop part is your secondary name?

Mr. Welling: Objected to as calling for a conclusion.

(Sustained. Exception.)

Q. But the point of your particular act during the past few months, or in 1933, you did employ the name "Mae Betty Boop Questal"; is that correct?

A. Yes.

Q. Is Questal your correct name?

A. Yes.

Q. What is your age (—I do not mean to be personal)?

A. I am over 21.

Q. Did you ever mimic Helen Kane?

A. Yes, I did.

Q. When you mimicked her, you sang "That's My Weakness Now"; isn't that correct?

A. I sang "He's So Unusual."

Q. Did you also sing "That's My Weakness Now"; don't you remember that?

A. In the cartoon.

Q. In the cartoon when you mimicked Helen Kane and sang "That's My Weakness Now"?

A. I did not mimic Helen Kane.

Q. In the question I asked you a few moments ago, I asked you whether in your personal appearance you mimicked Helen Kane, and you said yes; is that correct?

A. Yes.

Q. Then I asked you whether in mimicking Helen Kane you sang "That's My Weakness Now," and you said, "No, in cartoons I sang 'That's My Weakness Now.'" Isn't that correct?

A. I sang the song.

Q. "That's My Weakness Now"?

A. Yes.

Q. That is when you mimicked Helen Kane?

A. No.

Q. Do you remember where you saw Miss Helen Kane before you entered this Fordham impersonation contest?

A. Yes.

Q. You saw Miss Kane at the Paramount during her six weeks stay there, didn't you?

A. I do.

Q. Do you remember her singing to Paul Ash "That's My Weakness Now"?

A. I do.

Q. She sang it rather cutely, didn't she?

A. I think so.

Q. It made quite an impression on you—you seem to hesitate?

A. It did.

Q. How many times did you go to see Miss Helen Kane at the Paramount when she sang "That's My Weakness Now" to Paul Ash; three or four times?

A. I did not go to see Miss Kane. I went to the theatre only once.

Q. But coincidentally you saw Miss Kane?

A. Yes.

Q. When you sang in the boop-boop-a-doop contest at the Fordham Theatre, did you sing "That's My Weakness Now'?

A. No.

Q. You sang "He's So Unusual"?

A. Yes.

Q. Did you sing this song, "Stopping the Show"—the cartoon "Stopping the Show"?

A. I made the cartoon.

Q. In that cartoon you purported to imitate three different characters; isn't that true?

A. Just two.

Q. Do you remember that when you sang Maurice Chevalier, that is, an imitation of him, a photograph of Maurice Chevalier was put on the cartoon?

A. Yes.

Q. And his name was mentioned; is that right?

A. Yes.

Q. And you sang "Hello, Beautiful"?

A. I did.

Q. And before singing Maurice Chevalier's "Hello, Beautiful," you sang "I am an Indian," in imitation of Fannie Brice?

A. Yes.

Q. And then they put a picture on of Fannie Brice?

A. Yes.

Q. Before that you sang in imitation of Betty Boop and they put up the name Betty Boop, with her picture in the cartoon; isn't that correct?

A. I don't remember seeing that.

Q. Do you remember that you were supposed to sing "That's My Weakness Now" in imitation of Betty Boop; is that right?

A. Right.

Q. So that you did three imitations in that song, "Stopping the Show," is that correct?

A. No, not exactly.

Q. Miss Questal, where else did you see Miss Kane perform?

A. The night I won the contest, in the theatre.

Q. That was an impersonal contest of Helen Kane,

wasn't it?

A. That was a Helen Kane contest.

Q. It was a contest where people were impersonating Helen Kane and the best impersonator won the prize?

A. I don't know about impersonations.

Q. At the Riverside Theatre, you think that it was a boop-boop-a-doop contest when you won the $100 prize?

A. It was a Helen Kane contest.

Q. And the girls who sang, sang in imitation of Helen Kane; is that so?

A. Yes.

Q. Wasn't that true at the Fordham Theatre?

A. Yes.

Q. What song did you sing at the Riverside Theatre?

A. "He's So Unusual."

Q. You sang that again?

A. Yes.

Q. And you sang that because you knew Helen Kane was popular for that song?

A. I learned the song to imitate—

Q. You learned the song to imitate Helen Kane?

A. For the contest.

Q. In learning the song to imitate Helen Kane; you listened to her sing that in the movies in order to imitate her character?

A. I saw the picture once.

Q. In order to imitate her you observed her characteristics, didn't you?

A. Yes.

Q. And you observed her gesticulations of the hands, didn't you? Yes or no.

A. I do not think so.

Q. Did you observe the melody that she put into her song?

A. Yes.

Q. Did you observe the way she sang "boop-boop-a-doop"; do you remember that?

A. I don't remember that picture.

Q. You remember the way that she sang the "boop-boop-a-doop" in interpolations in the "That's My

Weakness Now" at the Paramount?

A. Yes.

Q. And when you sang at the Fordham you used "boop-boop-a-doop" in interpolations, didn't you?

A. Yes.

Q. And likewise at the Riverside, didn't you?

A. Yes.

Q. And you knew that Helen Kane was the "boop-boop-a-doop Girl"; isn't that so?

Mr. Welling: I object to the question.

Mr. Weltz: Question withdrawn.

Q. When were you first employed after the Helen Kane contest? By whom were you employed?

A. R.K.O.

Q. In the act that you did in imitation of Helen Kane?

A. Yes.

Q. You were introduced as Mae Questal, the winner of the Helen Kane impersonal "boop-boop-a-doop" contest; isn't that true?

A. No.

Q. What was it?

A. Mae Questal, the winner of Helen Kane tri-borough contest.

Q. You were the winner of the three-boroughs contest?

A. Yes.

Q. That is, the Bronx, Brooklyn, and Manhattan?

A. Yes, sir.

Q. You do your hair, or you have your hair combed like Miss Kane; isn't that true?

A. I have always had this hair combed this way.

Q. But you have it now combed like Miss Helen Kane?

A. I don't know.

Q. Will you take off your hat; you have spit curls on the side and the forehead like Miss Kane; is that right?

A. I think so.

Q. Do you know that Margy Hines has her hair done that way, too?

Mr. Welling: Objected to.

A. I don't know.

Q. I will show you the photograph; I want to show you the coincidence.

The Court: No; you must proceed with questions.

Q. Did you ever see Bonnie Poe?

A. Yes.

Q. Bonnie Poe has her hair combed like Miss Kane did?

A. Up to date.

Q. When you saw her she did?

A. Yes.

Q. You say that you always wore your hair with the curls on the forehead and on the cheeks; is that right?

A. Yes.

Q. Have you any photographs that were taken of you before you entered the Helen Kane amateur contest?

A. I don't know.

Q. Perhaps I can show you one; do you recognize this picture (showing witness paper)?

A. Yes.

Q. That is a picture of you when you won the contest; isn't that right?

A. No.

Q. Just a little before the contest?

A. About a year after the contest.

Q. Where was this picture taken?

A. At the White Studio, on 42nd Street, I think.

Q. Have you any pictures of you that were taken in 1928?

A. I do not think so.

Q. What songs did you sing in imitation of Helen Kane on the stage after you went into the impersonal contest?

A. The same songs.

Q. What is that song?

A. "He's So Unusual."

Q. What else—"That's My Weakness Now"?

A. No.

Q. What else?

A. "Black and Blue Blues."

Q. I show you Plaintiff's Exhibit 40 in evidence, of the song "That's My Weakness Now"; do you notice the picture of Helen Kane on that?

A. Yes.

Q. Did you ever see this song, "That's My Weakness

Now," in the song sheet Plaintiff's Exhibit 401?

A. Yes.

Q. 1928, did you see it?

A. No.

Q. Did you hear any records of Miss Kane?

A. I don't think so.

Q. Where else did you see Miss Kane before the Fordham contest?

A. In the movies.

Q. In person, I mean?

A. At the Fordham Theatre.

Q. Before the Fordham Theatre?

A. I don't think I did.

Q. Did you hear Miss Kane sing "That's My Weakness Now" at the Fordham?

A. No.

Q. You only heard her sing it at the Paramount?

A. Yes.

Q. That is the only song that she sang when you saw her at the Paramount?

A. I think she sang another song, but I am not sure.

Q. Do you remember that she sang "Is There Anything Wrong in That" at the Paramount?

A. Maybe.

Q. Do you remember that the other two girls who won the "boop-boop-a-doop" tri-borough contest sang "Do Something"?

A. It was the Helen Kane contest.

Q. We will call it the Helen Kane contest. Do you remember while you were billed at the R.K.O. at one time when you were billed as Mae Questal, the winner of the Helen Kane contest, your name was in small print and Miss Kane's in very large print; do you remember that?

A. No.

Mr. Welling: Objected to. (Overruled. Exception.)

Q. Isn't it a fact that originally when you first appeared at the R.K.O. you were billed as the prize-winner of, the boop-boop-a-doop of the tri-borough Helen Kane impersonal contest?

A. I don't remember being billed like that.

Q. If I show you this clipping, do you think that it may

refresh your recollection (indicating)?

A. No.

Q. Now, do you remember?

A. I don't remember of being billed that way in the theatres.

Q. Where were you billed that way?

A. No where.

Q. Did you ever read that clipping—I will withdraw that. Did you ever hear of the New York Billboard?

A. Yes.

Q. Theatrical magazine?

A. Yes.

Q. Did you ever read that clipping of the New York Billboard, a theatrical magazine?

A. I just read it.

Q. Do you recall that after a while you became publicized as "The R.K.O. Find of the RKO."?

A. Yes.

Q. First you had been billed as the winner of the tri-borough Helen Kane personal contest?

A. Winner of the Helen Kane tri-borough contest.

Q. I refer to the impersonal contest?

A. I refer to the Helen Kane contest.

Q. Didn't it refer to the impersonal contest?

A. I do not think so.

Q. After a while that was changed to the R.K.O. Find?

A. Yes.

Q. What other singer did you imitate in your mimicking during the theatrical appearances that you made?

A. Irene Bordoni.

Q. What song is she famous for?

Mr. Phillips: I object to the form of the question.

Q. What song did you sing?

A. I sang "There Is Danger in Your Eyes, Cherie."

Q. Did you know that was the song that Irene Bordoni had sung?

A. No. I only saw Miss Bordoni sing it once.

Q. Do you keep abreast of the theatrical things that occur?

A. As much as I can.

Q. You are quite an educated young lady; you read quite a bit?

A. Yes.

Q. Don't you know that Irene Bordoni is known for her singing of that song that you just mentioned? (Objected to. Sustained.)

Q. When you sang in impersonation of Irene Bordoni, did you attempt to sing in the same style in which Irene Bordoni sang?

Mr. Welling: Objected to. (Overruled. Exception.)

A. I tried to.

Q. Did you try to use her intonations and her expressions in the imitation?

A. Only intonations.

Q. Didn't you also try to use her form of rhythm and melody—do you know what I mean?

A. No.

Q. When you sing in imitation of Maurice Chevalier, do you try to use the rhythm that he uses?

A. I try to exaggerate the things.

Q. In order to exaggerate you have to know the things that he does, don't you?

A. Yes.

Q. Did you try to exaggerate Irene Bordoni's method of singing?

A. Yes.

Q. Then you must have known her mannerisms?

A. Yes.

Q. And you must have known a little of the melody or the rhythm that she puts into her songs?

A. That is not very outstanding about Miss Bordoni.

Q. What is outstanding about her?

A. Her French accent and her gestures.

Q. And those you accentuated?

A. Yes.

Q. When you impersonated Helen Kane, what characterization did you mimic or exaggerate?

A. Her face.

Q. Was it the rolling of her eyes?

A. No.

Q. What else?

A. Her gestures.

Q. Was it the way she sang boop-boop-a-doop; wasn't that one of the things, too?

A. I sang boop-boop-a-doop in the song.

Q. Didn't you try to sing it the way that Helen Kane would sing boop-boop-a-doop?

A. I sang it a little differently.

Q. But in intonations of Helen Kane

Mr. Phillips: Objected to as incompetent, irrelevant and immaterial. She said that she sang it differently. (Overruled. Exception.)

A. (No answer.)

Q. In singing the boop-boop-a-doop interpolations in imitation of Helen Kane, didn't you endeavor to sing it as Helen Kane sang it; isn't that true?

A. Yes.

Q. What other songs did you sing of Helen Kane?

A. In imitation of her, that is the only one I sang in imitation of Helen Kane.

Q. When you said that you tried to imitate her face, didn't you mean by that her facial expression!

A. Her pout.

Q. When you say pout, you mean the pushing forward of the lips?

A. Yes.

Q. The pout that people knew her for; is that right?

Mr. Welling: Objected to.

Mr. Weltz: Question withdrawn.

Q. What else did you do facially other than Miss Kane's pout?

A. I don't know.

Q. You don't know?

A. I never study my own face in the mirror.

Q. I presume that is so. I do not question it; without looking in the mirror cannot you tell us how you make the imitation, your facial expression, I mean?

A. No.

Q. When you imitate Maurice Chevalier, did you imitate the facial mannerism for which he is well known?

A. As much as I could, yes.

Q. All of these prominent actors or actresses have certain characteristics that you try to bring out in your imitation; isn't that so?

A. I try to exaggerate.

Q. In your exaggeration you are anxious for people to recognize or identify the person whom you are mimicking?

A. I think every imitator does.

Q. I am talking about you, particularly.

A. Yes.

Q. I am not concerned with anybody else; is that right?

A. Yes.

Q. You say you were first billed with the R.K.O. as the winner of the Helen Kane tri-borough contest; is that correct?

A. Yes.

Q. And before the winning of that contest, which was at the Riverside; is that correct?

A. There was one at the Fordham, too.

Q. The tri-borough contest?

A. Oh, yes, at the Riverside.

Q. I think you got $100 in gold from Miss Kane?

A. Yes.

Q. Before that, was your first appearance the appearance that you made at the Fordham, theatrically?

A. No.

Q. Had you appeared theatrically before the Fordham appearance?

A. Yes.

Q. Professionally?

A. No.

Q. When I talk of the Fordham appearance, of course you understand I am referring to the Helen Kane personal contest at Fordham, do you know that?

A. Yes.

Q. After that contest, which you won, you received a booking for the first time; isn't that right?

A. Yes.

Q. And in your booking right after that contest you were also booked as the winner of the Fordham Helen Kane impersonal contest; is that correct?

A. I was booked as the winner of the Helen Kane tri-borough contest.

Q. You did appear first at the Fordham for the Fordham-Helen Kane contest; is that correct?

A. Yes.

Q. Before that appearance you had never appeared professionally; isn't that correct?

A. Yes.

Q. And for that appearance you received the four-day booking; is that correct?

A. Yes.

Q. And during that booking you did impersonations of Helen Kane, didn't you?

A. Just one song.

Q. Only one song?

A. Yes.

Q. What was that song?

A. "He's So Unusual."

Q. That was four days—what theater?

A. Fordham Theatre.

Q. At the Fordham you were introduced or advertised as the winner of the Fordham-Helen Kane contest; isn't that right?

A. Yes.

Q. And after that you went into the tri-borough contest?

A. Yes.

Q. And there were only three girls who were in the tri-borough contest; is that right?

A. Yes.

Q. When did you start singing for the Betty Boop cartoon?

A. I think about the year 1931.

Q. What is that?

A. I am not sure of the date.

Mr. Phillips: I ask to have these documents marked for identification.

(16 papers marked Defendants' Exhibit KK for Identification.)

Recess until 2 P. M. May 4, 1934.

Many newspapers reported on May 5, 1934, that Helen Kane lost the trial. Judge McGoldrick ruled that Helen had failed to prove her contention that the defendants wrongfully appropriated her singing technique in the Betty Boop film cartoons. "I consider it very unfair as all my friends believe the cartoons are a deliberate caricature of me," she said in an interview.

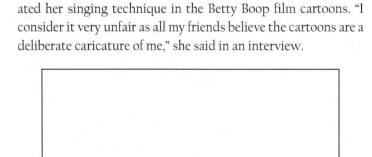

From the left: Kate Wright, Little Ann Rothschild aka Little Ann Little, Mae Questel, Margie Hines, and Bonnie Poe, with Max Fleischer sitting in the center.

Immediately following the trial, Max Fleischer assembled Mae Questel, Margie Hines, Ann Little, Kate Wright, and Bonnie Poe to record a very short video, often labeled a victory reel, that was well under a minute. Mae took the lead as they all sang, "Don't take our boop-boop-a-doop away!" as Max sat in front of the five ladies. Story has it that the reason for the victory newsreel was that during the trial, Helen Kane ignored the other voices of Betty Boop and pretended they were not there, so this short was their response to her. This reel features Mae Questel singing the leading role because she was the most popular voice of Betty Boop.

Not long after, ads began appearing in newspapers with headlines such as "Max Fleischer Comedies Presents in Person - Mae Questel - in Person, Positively the Original Betty Boop Girl," and "Miss Betty Boop–Mae Questel and other Acts." Mae Questel was not experiencing a decline in popularity, and the demand for her to promote products other than for Fleischer Studios grew.

As Mae was enjoying an additional rise in popularity and with the ever-increasing popularity of Popeye, Betty Boop, through no fault of her own, began to slide in popularity after about 1934. In 1930, the Motion Picture Production Code was adopted by the Association of Motion Picture Producers Inc. to maintain social and community values in the production of silent, synchronized, and talking pictures.

The advent of sound with motion pictures brought new problems of self-discipline and regulation to the motion picture industry, and it became necessary to reaffirm the standards under which silent films had been produced since 1922. Basically, the purpose of the code was to officially enforce many rules established in Hollywood by various studios since about 1930 and to create standards that would enable them to avoid official government censorship and to appease the constantly growing concerns that motion pictures were immoral entertainment.

Primarily fueled by the American Catholic Church, there was a danger that government censorship would seize control of the film industry, and changes were made by 1934. These were the years of scantily-clad flapper girls, violent crime dramas, and horror films such as *Frankenstein* and *Dracula* with nudity and sexual content often being expressed, especially by Mae West, and of course, Betty Boop became one of the names often brought up because many found a cartoon character with cleavage and a high skirt with exposed garter belt offensive. One reference mentioned, "Betty Boop is a filthy, immoral hussy, corrupting our children!"

To silence the many critics, under the "Hays Code," as it is sometimes called, homosexuality, interracial romance, drug and alcohol use, abortion, and nudity were now prohibited. Couples could not be seen sharing a bed, violence was toned down, and stories in which good and evil were confused were prohibited. An evil character could not, at all, be portrayed in a way as to gain sympathy from the audience and must be punished before the film is over. This code remained in effect until 1960.

The Production Code of 1934 forced Fleischer Studios to change its golden girl. One account mentions that intimidation tactics were utilized to motivate Fleischer Studios into complying with the new code. By today's standards the code is rather absurd, but Betty Boop was clearly an offender of the code because her sexy teases contained "too much promise." As a result, Betty's hemline was lowered, her garter belt disappeared, now only her calves were revealed; and her healthy cleavage disappeared. Instead of playing dance-hall characters, she was typecast as a schoolmarm. The adventures she very often had with Bimbo and Koko were also deemed inappropriate, and Betty was paired with cute animals and children who seemed to follow standards laid out by Disney instead of the characters who would often lustily pursue Betty, but it was clear that Fleischer Studios only portrayed these events as a tease.

Betty Boop was doomed, and her last cartoon was in 1939. From that point on, Betty Boop disappeared from movie screens, and Mae Questel's voice would not be heard again as Betty Boop for many years. Nevertheless, Mae was certainly not out of work and remained busy with voice work in the popular Popeye cartoons. Although Popeye was regarded as violent, the sailorman did not drink or talk suggestively, and Olive Oyl (voiced by Mae Questel) was unlikely to inspire erotic emotions in those who watched her on the screen.

Mae continued to make Betty Boop appearances in and around the New York area as others such as Boris Karloff performed in the *Bride of Frankenstein,* and W. C. Fields and the young Bing Crosby entertained audiences across the states. Interestingly, I reviewed several articles from various newspapers around the country that asked if Helen Kane and Mae Questel were "one in the same." Mae's popularity was spreading, and she began to endorse more products as more people came to know her name. One such example is this ad from a New York paper:

"A Late Snack Brings Sleep to Betty Boop." It requires a lot of energy to keep going all the time like little Mae (Betty Boop) Questel, the voice of Betty Boop, screen character. Mae herself, on or off the stage, is as vivacious as the screen Betty Boop. Her laugh and merry brown eyes are just as infectiously captivating.

"I keep busy, of course, but I'm strong and healthy and I suppose that is because my mother takes good care of me," Mae explains, and in offering this explanation she undoubtedly gives credit where credit is due. Her mother is of the sensible, old-fashioned type whose every thought is for her daughter's health and happiness. Her mother plans her other meals, too, taking care to choose the foods that promote health and energy. A bran nut bread falls in this class and below is a recipe for it. [November 1, 1934, *New York Black River Democrat*, pg 2.]

Everything was progressing well at Fleischer Studios, and it appeared that everyone was happy. Unionization had been discussed between a few employees, but no real interest was stirred. In April 1935 all the personnel at Fleischer Studios received a pamphlet from the Animated Motion Picture Workers Union that told everyone to rise up, take over the studio, and demand better working conditions, higher wages, and shorter work hours, none of which anyone within the studio had complaints about. This did eventually fizzle, but a few of the lower-paid employees continued to discuss it among themselves.

Union activity gained a great deal of momentum when the Wagner Labor Relation Act was passed in July 1935, giving workers the right to organize and make demands without owner interference. Outside influences continued to push employees of Fleischer Studios. Eventually, this caused a split within the studio, and the family-like atmosphere began to evaporate. Times were changing.

With tensions high at Fleischer Studios, Mae took an opportunity to travel to California to the MGM Studios in Culver City to provide a voice characterization in a short they were producing, *New Shoes*, released on September 5, 1936. The film short begins in a busy metropolitan city and quickly closes in on the front of a shoe store. Then a woman chooses a pair of shoes from in the storefront. Then a man chooses a pair of shoes from the storefront. The scene changes back to the woman's shoes, which all begin to sing "time to meet the dangers of the street," and a pair of light-colored shoes with bows begins to sing (voice by Mae Questel) about walking. Then it is the men's shoes' turn to sing (voice by Billy Bletcher); then all the shoes sing about romance.

To help the audience follow which shoe is singing, the bows on the woman's shoes will move and either the laces or the tongue will move on the men's shoes.

The scene changes to the inside of the shoe store, where sales staff scurry around helping customers, when one of the pair of women's shoes is sitting next to one of the men's pair of shoes on the floor. Then the focus moves up to a young woman (played by Jean Chatburn) sitting in a chair and a young man (played by Arthur Lake, later known for his role of Dagwood in the Blondie and Dagwood films) sitting in a chair next to her. He is trying his best to get the young woman's attention; she appears to be thinking of something else but is politely ignoring him.

Then the focus returns to the floor, where the man's shoe tells the woman's shoe that he's "taking a shine to you." The woman's shoe responds, "You hold your tongue, you heel!" He responds, "You're nothing but a high heel yourself." The scene switches back to the man and woman sitting in the chairs. The man continues to attempt a conversation, but the woman brushes him off. They purchase their new shoes, and as they begin to leave the store, the man asks the woman to dinner, but he is brushed off again.

Later, the pair of women's and of men's shoes are seen exiting a rather luxurious looking car and are soon dancing, while a band is playing, as the man and woman are also dancing with each other. The two pairs of shoes are soon seen smoking from all the dancing, and the man and woman exchange rather painful looks from their uncomfortable shoes. As soon as the band stops, they take a break. The woman's shoes are now panting, and as the woman removes her feet from the shoes, they say, "That is a relief." Then the man's shoes say, "He gave me an awful lacing." The woman's shoes say that it is a wonderful night for romance and how nice it is to be "with you alone here under the table." The man's shoes respond, "Stop it; you're breaking my arch." As the man and the woman are enjoying a little romance above the table, they break out into a song, the same song as the band was singing when they were dancing. The scene ends as they kiss.

In the next scene, the woman is receiving a foot massage from her maid when the telephone rings. She answers and hears the man singing the same song. He has his feet in two buckets of ice water and continues singing to the woman over the telephone. The short ends with a "just married" sign on the back of a car. Their shoes are tied to the bumper with tin cans, and then the couple drives away. The running time for this short is 10:20, and it is in black-and-white.

Shortly after the release of *New Shoes*, *Popeye the Sailor Meets Ali Baba's Forty Thieves* was released on November 26, 1937. Mae provided voice characterization for Olive Oyl in the two-reel cartoon produced in Technicolor and utilized Fleischer Studios' multiplane camera, which the studio had been working with for a while. Additionally, in the cave scene, the studio had a chance to show its tabletop 3D ground process. This was the second of three cartoons over sixteen minutes for the Popeye series and was released as Disney was entering its final months of production on its first animated feature, *Snow White and the Seven Dwarfs*.

CHAPTER 3. 1937–1966

By 1937, the media was filled with news of strikes including the United Auto Workers, the Blind Workers Union, the Teamsters, and the "Memorial Day Massacre" on 30 May when ten unarmed demonstrators of the Steel Workers Organizing Committee were killed by the Chicago police; that had the whole country talking about unions.

Max Fleischer was approached by a small delegation of employees with some complaints such as no paid sick leave, no paid vacations, and their wanting a forty-hour workweek. Max did not pay much attention, believing that was only a very small percentage of employees. But he was wrong, and the Commercial Artists' and Designers' Union (CADU) had persuaded about one hundred of Fleischer Studios employee's to join, and soon after they approached Max again.

Max not only did not negotiate with the union, but he also refused to recognize it, and eventually a strike was voted in. Some picket signs said humorous things like, "We can't get much spinach on salaries as low as $15.00." When about five nonstrikers returned to the studio after dinner, they found strikers singing, "I'm Popeye the Union Man." When the nonstrikers attempted to cross the picket line, a fight broke out. The police arrived, and it turned into a brawl that lasted about an hour and a half, with several arrested; the incident attracted about two thousand New Yorkers.

The strike lasted about six months without further violence. It is not clear if Mae was involved, but because she was not a "full-time" employee, she may not have had to choose sides. She did continue to voice Betty Boop, Olive Oyl and other voices in the cartoons produced during the strike. Mae also took on outside work during the period of unrest at Fleischer Studios, and she performed in *The Great Ziegfeld*, which was released on March 22, 1936, and shot at the MGM Studios in Culver City, California. *The Great Ziegfeld* is a fictionalized tribute to Florenz Ziegfeld Jr., and the film is best often remembered for the highly elaborate costumes, dances, and complex revolving sets. The costumes in themselves required 250 tailors and seamstresses and about six months to prepare them. One estimate gives an account that one thousand people were employed in the production of the film. Acclaimed as one of the biggest successes in film at the time, it was the pride of MGM. It was also heralded as the greatest musical biography to be made in Hollywood and remains a standard in musical filmmaking, winning three Academy Awards.

Mae's role was very minor, however. Ziegfeld tries to make a star out of Audrey Dane, who is plagued with alcoholism, and he lures Fanny Price away from vaudeville. In this scene, Fanny introduces different burlesque girls, each with her own dancing style. First there is Dolly, then Molly, and then Rosie (played by Mae Questel), who sings "I'm fancy free" before she exits the stage as quickly as she had entered.

Although the film is still viewed as a symbol of glamour and excess during what is coined as the golden age of Hollywood, it is now criticized for the actors overacting and for being too long (more than three hours). Nevertheless, anyone wishing to learn a little about the showman Florenz Ziegfeld or the period in which he lived would enjoy this film.

In November 1936, Mae began doing radio work on the *Jack Pearl Show*, which was carried by the Blue Network. (The Blue

Network and its predecessor, the NBC Blue Network, were names of the now defunct American Radio Production and Distribution that operated from 1927 to 1945). Jack Pearl played a character commonly known as Baron Munchausen on the short-lived show of only twenty-eight episodes. Mae appeared in the first nine shows, with the first airing November 23, 1936, and the last on November 18, 1937 (Appendix 1 contains all her air-dates and the characters she performed on the show). Basically, Mae supported Jack Pearl's character, which was based on the exploits of the fictional character Baron von Munchausen, an officer in the eighteenth-century German cavalry who in his later years wrote of his wildest adventures.

The show was set up in a vaudeville style with a straight man (or woman, like Mae Questel) feeding setup lines and Jack (the baron) punching them with witty comebacks. An example would be when the baron is asked if "He is still at Penn State?" and the baron replies, "No, now he iss in der state pen and he's going to die," in his best German accent.

The Germans and Germany were becoming more common subjects in the news at the time. On May 3, 1937 the German airship *Hindenburg* departed Frankfurt, Germany, bound for Lakehurst, New Jersey. At 7:21 p.m. on May 6, while attempting to dock at the Lakehurst Naval Air Station, the *Hindenburg* burst into flames, killing thirty-five passengers and crew and one ground-crew member. Public confidence was shattered as a result and this marked the end of an era for rigid airship travel.

After numerous strikes in the auto industry, General Motors was forced to recognize the UAW (United Auto Workers). The Steel Workers Organizing Committee, the precursor to the United Steelworkers, signed a collective bargaining agreement with U.S. Steel. At this time, the Supreme Court of the United States ruled that the National Relations Act was constitutional.

Max Fleischer never did acknowledge the union and maintained that anyone could work for the studio without being a CADU member. In addition to the release of the first feature-length Technicolor cartoon *Snow White and the Seven Dwarfs* by

Disney Studios, and the release of the animated short *Porky's Duck Hunt* on April 17, 1937 (directed by Tex Avery for the Looney Tunes series and featuring the debut of Daffy Duck), Max began to rethink the future of Fleischer Studios, which had been tainted by the strike. Max had wanted to do a feature-length cartoon, but Paramount did not support the idea until the release from Disney Studios. Now Paramount wanted a feature-length cartoon, and Fleischer Studios was excited, but the present studio at 1600 Broadway was too small to house the number of additional personnel required to produce the cartoon. Max turned to Miami, Florida, where he knew several city council members who offered many incentives to move the studio to their city.

On May 27, 1938, using the entire library of already-produced cartoons as collateral, Max signed a deal with Paramount ratifying the loan that would finance the move. Max offered all his employees a very attractive package that would move them, their families, and their relatives with all expenses paid, including temporary housing and shipping of their belongings. Max went as far as to promise to move them back to New York if they wanted to leave Miami. About 250 employees accepted the offer, but Mae Questel did not and chose to remain in New York with her family. At the time of the signing of the contract, she was about seven to eight months pregnant with her second son.

By 1937, Fleischer Studios and Disney saw Leon Schlesinger Productions put a group of new animated characters on the screen. Schlesinger was, at that time, already producing Merrie Melodies and had just released Looney Tunes, and by the end of that decade, their characters were globally popular. Porky Pig, Daffy Duck, and Bugs Bunny soon surpassed anything from Disney and Universal Studios as the three most successful characters in animated shorts.

As Looney Tunes gained popularity, Betty Boop was just hanging on, but Popeye was still popular, and Mae continued to voice Betty Boop cartoons as well as Olive Oyl during the construction of the new Miami studio. On November 10, 1937, Mae recorded "In our Little Wooden Shoes" and "I Want You for

Christmas" with Louis Armstrong on a Decca record.

Based on Mae's account, she last performed a Betty Boop voice on July 7, 1939. There are suggestions that Mae last performed in the Popeye cartoons on November 18, 1939, and did not perform again until Jack Mercer was called to serve during World War II. During that time, she performed in between eight and ten Popeye cartoons, providing Popeye's voice (based on her own accounts), in addition to Olive Oyl's, with the first appearing on May 26, 1944, and the last appearing on April 27, 1945.

Mae's work with voicing in the Popeye series took a break from November 1938 until May 1939. On February 10, 1940, Mae, "the original boop-boop-a-doop girl," appeared on the *Major Bowes Family*, which, at the time, was a national radio program with studios in New York. The amateur talent contest attracted as many as ten thousand people a week who applied to the show, but most were turned away. Five to seven hundred were auditioned, and only about twenty appeared on the show. Many people sold their homes, hitched rides, and traveled any way they could for a chance to be on the New York show. Even after making the show, many were "gonged" off before finishing their acts, a cruel practice that made audiences hysterical with laughter. A few exceptions included Frank Sinatra, Beverly Sills, and Paul Winchell. The show made Major Bowes a very wealthy man, and the show remained very popular until his death in 1946. The show did continue into the 1950s but with little success.

The events unfolding in Europe and Japan dominated the news, and tensions between the United States and Germany increased when a German submarine fired on a US ship on September 4, 1941. When Japan attacked Pearl Harbor on December 7, 1941, the United States was drawn into the war, and the following day, President Roosevelt officially declared war on Japan. Three days later, Germany and Italy declared war on the United States.

Not long after, almost everyone turned his or her efforts toward supporting the war effort, and the entertainment industry was no different. It was certainly an important part of the

American propaganda. The movie-going experience often included a newsreel that lasted about 10 minutes giving accounts of battles against the enemy, followed by a cartoon. Among these titles were *Japoteurs* (1942) featuring Superman, *Der Fuehrer's Face* (1943) starring Donald Duck, *Confessions of a Nutsy Spy* (1943) with Bugs Bunny, and *Daffy the Commando* (1943) with Daffy Duck. Many of these "banned" cartoons are available to watch on websites such as Youtube.

While studios like Disney and Warner Brothers were producing cartoons for the war effort, Fleischer Studios did not, and in 1942, Paramount seized control of the studio and ousted Max and Dave Fleischer. Personal and professional disputes between Max and Dave Fleischer began taking a toll on the studio. Given with the studio's dwindling profits and frequent loans from Paramount, Paramount was eventually forced to recall their loans and for the resignations of the brothers. They turned Fleischer Studios over to Paramount. On May 25, 1942, Paramount officially founded Famous Studios, and several former Fleischer Studios employees remained to fill top positions. Jack Mercer (the voice of Popeye) and Mae Questel continued to supply voice characterizations.

Famous Studios began producing Popeye cartoons in Technicolor, a major transition from black-and-white, and Noveltoons was launched, again utilizing Mae's voice talents.

On June 26, 1943, the first Private Snafu ("snafu" is an acronym for Situation Normal All Fouled [another expletive is sometimes used] Up) produced by Leon Schlesinger and voiced by Mel Blanc, premiered. The films were designed to instruct service personnel about various issues such as security, proper sanitation and hygiene, booby traps and other military subjects, and, of course, improving troop morale. Their goal was to help enlisted men with weak literacy skills learn through animated cartoons. At the time Private Snafu cartoons were a military secret and were regarded as classified government documents.

Beginning in 1943, Paramount Pictures' Famous Studios produced Noveltoons, which in essence was an anthology series of animated cartoons that included Casper the Friendly Ghost, Herman and Katnip, Little Lulu, Little Audrey, and Baby Huey, and Mae provided many of those voices. I have attempted to include these in appendices 3, 5 and 6. This series was similar in nature to Warner Brothers' Looney Tunes and Merrie Melodies.

By the end of 1943, the war in Europe was slowly beginning to turn in the favor of the Allies, and cautious talk of Victory began to spread. In this atmosphere, the radio program *Atlantic Spotlight* was produced for NBC Radio in conjunction with the BBC (British Broadcast Company). Premiering on January 1, 1944, *Atlantic Spotlight* was broadcast simultaneously in the United States and Great Britain and, as much as possible, forwarded on to the Allied Troops. The program featured guest emcees in both New York and London. Considering Mae's other work with NBC, it was not difficult for her to accept an invitation to appear in support of the war effort. Mae Questel joined with performers Clive Richardson, Tony Lowry, Harry Hemsley, Leslie Mitchell, and Malcolm Sargeant in an episode that aired Saturday at 12:30 p.m. on March 10, 1945, and ran for thirty minutes. This is perhaps the only episode of *Atlantic Spotlight* that Mae appeared in; no other records that mention her appearance have been located.

A brief description of the show in the Library of Congress Records indicates that it seems to be closely associated with the American Theater Wing's *Stage Door Canteen*. The original canteen was set up by the Wing as a service to servicemen. Actors and other theater people would work in the canteen, serving and even doing kitchen duties to support the GIs and Allied soldiers passing through. The canteen idea spread during the war, with similar facilities opening in other cities, including the famous Hollywood Canteen, which featured many movie personalities who were also hard at work supporting Armed Forces Radio Service programs like *Command Performance* and *G.I. Journal*. The series ended on February 2, 1946.

By 1944, the Germans were losing ground and beginning to pull back toward Germany. On 6 June 1944, more than 160,000 allied troops landed along a fifty-mile stretch of heavily fortified

French coastline to fight Nazi Germany.

On May 26, 1944, Mae resumed working, providing voices for the Popeye series, primarily as Olive Oyl. Although Mae only voiced five Popeye cartoons for 1944, Noveltoons did produce a few cartoons with a war theme/support. Mae only provided voices for four Popeye cartoons the following year of 1945.

An Associated Press (AP) article from New York reported that Mae Questel helped Robert "Q" Lewis launch his new radio comedy show *Listen to Lewis*, more commonly called *The Robert Q. Lewis Show*. Robert Lewis was best known as a horned-rimmed-glasses-wearing comic that in his early career began as a fill-in in an early-morning NBC slot but was fired for telling jokes about the network vice president. Mae appeared as a guest star on his first show, which aired on Saturday, April 7, 1945, with variety music performed by the Murphy Sisters and the Dave Grupp Orchestra. The show lasted exactly three months. That year saw many very important events, such as Hitler and Eva Braun committing suicide on April 30, followed by V-E (Victory in Europe), May 8, on which Germany unconditionally surrendered. On August 6, American forces dropped an atomic bomb on the city of Hiroshima followed by another on Nagasaki, which led to V-J (Victory in Japan), the unconditional surrender of Japan and the end of World War II.

Mae was also busy with a new project by Famous Studios, Little Lulu. Little Lulu began as a comic strip character debuting in the *Saturday Evening Post* on February 23, 1935, and ran until 1944. The first animated short by Famous Studio for Paramount, which replaced the Superman shorts, began on December 14, 1943. In all, twenty-six cartoon shorts were produced with Mae Questel providing the voice not only for Little Lulu but also for other characters in the cartoons. Paramount allowed the rights to expire, and the series was replaced by the Little Audrey cartoon with Mae retained to supply voices for those cartoons also. The last of the Little Lulu cartoon was released on January 30, 1948. Appendix 5 contains a list of the Little Lulu cartoons that Mae contributed to.

Little Audrey debuted in the Noveltoons *Santa's Surprise* on December 5, 1947, where she led a multicultural group of children who cleaned Santa's workshop while he was asleep. In all, sixteen cartoons starring Audrey were produced for theatrical release, several of which were repackaged for television from the late 1950s on. Little Audrey had a brief appearance in a January 1948 Popeye cartoon *Olive Oyl for President*, but no vocals were used.

Taking a break from cartoon voice characterizations, Mae was able to return to her first love: Broadway. The image shown is a very rare advertising handbill (fewer than one thousand were printed) that shows that Mae had traveled to Boston for a two-week pre-Broadway tryout of the play *Doctor Social* by Joseph L. Estry, which opened there on January 26, 1948, at the Plymouth Theatre. On February 11, 1948, Mae opened in her first legitimate Broadway play at the Booth Theatre on 45th Street, New York.

The three-act play took place in the office, laboratory, and treatment room of Dr. Norman Ferrar (played by Dean Jagger). Dr. Ferrar plans to sell a serum he developed for skin restoration to a commercial firm rather to a charitable foundation, much to the dissatisfaction of his old teacher. When Dr. Ferrar tests the serum on burn victim Lee Manning (played by Haila Stoddard), he discovers that it not only restores skin but that it also destroys cancer cells. When Dr. Ferrar falls in love with Lee, she convinces him to donate the formula to the charitable foundation.

In this play, Mae Questel played Yvonne Tompkins, who wanted her nose altered and then wondered whether, if she got married, the nose would crop up in her children again. A *New York Times* review called Mae's performance comical. Mae performed for the full production of three days, ending on February 14, 1948. The other performers were Ronald Alexander as Dr. Tom Morrisey, Donald Foster as Dr. Fleming, Eda Heinemann as Ann Harris, Al Shean as Dr. Isaac Gordon, and Nellie Malcolm as Mrs. Hamilton. The playbill mentions that the medical research depicted in the play stems in part from authentic scientific work reported in the October 10, 1947, issue of Science magazine.

Although Mae's career was prosperous, her private life was not, and it was time to remove a stressful influence from her life. Around this time, Mae divorced her first husband, Leo Balkin. Based on a couple of comments that Mae made later on, they did not part as friends, and a certain amount of bitterness could be detected in her comments. I will leave it at that. Mae quickly regained her luster, and it was not long before she was back in performance and made four appearances on the radio program *Stop Me If You've Heard this One*. The show was based on a panel of gag masters whose job was to expeditiously tell as many jokes as possible during the show so that the panel would attempt to interrupt and finish. Listeners were awarded prizes if the panel members were not able to complete the gag. According to newspaper accounts, Leon Janney was master of ceremonies at the time Mae appeared as a panelist on January 29, February 4, February 11, and February 18, 1949 carried by the NBC Network.

Mae had a single performance on the *Cavalcade of America*, which documents historical events and stories of American heroes from historical records from colonial days to the Revolution to the early 1900s. The show ran from 1935 to 1953, with it appearing on television in 1952. Mae played Patsy daughter of Thomas Jefferson in an episode that aired on January 10, 1949, titled "Experiment in Monticello," which tells how Thomas Jefferson proved the value of the smallpox vaccination by using the vaccine on his family, his servants, and his slaves. I was unable to locate Mae's name in other episodes, so it is safe to assume that she only appeared in this episode of the *Cavalcade of America*.

In October 1949, Mae appeared on the *Henry Morgan Show*. Henry Morgan was, at the time, known for his sarcastic comments about some of his sponsors. He so resented having to read the advertising in his show that he would not resist injecting his own remarks, often ridiculing the advertisers' claims, and lost many of his sponsors as a result. He is perhaps best remembered with the "Eversharp Schick Injector Razors." While reading a line he improvised, "They're educational. Try one. That'll teach you," and later appeared in *Life* magazine in a photo shoot with his face covered with bandages, praying to a razor.

Mae's only appearance on the *Henry Morgan Show* was on 14 October 1949, titled "Spoofs News Commentators" in which she performed in a skit about the two ways in which a movie star can be discovered. The skit unfolds like this: a producer enters a diner for his breakfast, and Mae's character asks him, "Want your eggs fried, boiled, or scrambled?" The producer, now very interested in her voice, asks her to repeat what she just said and asks her to remove her glasses, to wet her lips, and to throw out her chest. She repeats and the thrilled producer tells her to be in his office the following morning and to bring the eggs. In the second version of the skit, a different woman uses the same line, and the producer is not at all interested.

In mid-1949, NBC developed a radio program in which Mae would work with Tom Glazer. Titled *Tom, Timmy and Mae*, the musical variety show for children contained songs and stories, with Mae providing the voices of Timmy as an imaginary character throughout the series. The first airdate was on September 17, 1949, at 11:00 a.m., and as of October 29, 1949, it was broadcast at 9:00 a.m. on Saturday mornings. The program lasted until June 10, 1950. The show was abruptly canceled, and Tom Glazer would later contend that the "station manager wanted to show what a big patriot he was" because some observers had believed that there were communist connotations hidden in the show.

In the late 1940s and early 1950s, American fears of internal communist subversion reached a nearly hysterical pitch. Government loyalty boards investigated millions of federal employees, asking what books and magazines they read, what unions and civic organizations they belonged to, and whether they went to church. Hundreds of screenwriters, actors, and directors were blacklisted because of their alleged political beliefs while teachers, steelworkers, merchant sailors, lawyers, and social workers lost their jobs for similar reasons. More than thirty-nine states required teachers and other public employees to take loyalty oaths. Although the sentiment toward Tom Glazer hurt his career in the 1950s, it did not appear to have affected Mae Questel through association, or at least, nothing has been found. One broadcast record exists in the Library of Congress.

Mae performed in an animated Famous Studios Production called *Land of the Lost* released on June 7, 1949. Billy (voiced by Cecil Roy) and Isabel (voiced by Mae) are fishing from a small boat and catch a talking fish named the Red Lantern, who tells them to put some magic seaweed in their pockets so they can breathe under water. They soon arrive at a magic kingdom under water, Table Land, and then they go to the "Knives of the Square Table" to address the knives (voiced by Jack Mercer), who soon battle a villain. A jackknife that Billy had lost defeats the villain and is knighted. Then Billy and Isabel return to their small boat and tell the Red Lantern that they would like to see him again soon. And they do, in another episode called the *Land of the Lost Jewels*, released on January 6, 1950. Billy and Isabel are again fishing, and Isabel says that they will be lucky because she has her lucky pin "Hoppy-Go-Lucky" (a grasshopper), which she loses in the water as they catch the Red Lantern again. Red Lantern promises that she can retrieve her pin and tells the children to put magic seaweed in their pockets. They enter the underwater Land of the Lost to find Isabel's pin. Deemed a special jewel (Hoppy-Go-Lucky is made of emerald), it is tested and found to be only glass and is allowed to live in the Land of Toys. The episode ends like the first.

It is clear that Mae was able to move on with her life after her divorce, and an obscure article mentions that her ex-husband did also. Mae's former husband, Leo Balkin, woolen merchant on the new marriage certificate, married Bella Klein on March 18, 1950, in Manassas, Virginia. Leo's address at that time was on 23rd Street in New York, and Bella was from the Bronx. She was divorced and employed as a "buyer."

The last of the three Famous Studios Productions called *Land of Lost Watches* was released on May 4, 1951. With the same opening as the others, they visit the *Land of Lost Watches* and meet their father's lost timepiece that was separated from his sweetheart, Rosita Wristwatch, when he is sent to work in a clock hospital and she is sent to work in a circus. The two lovers are reunited when she is injured in an acrobatic routine and sent to her fiancé's hospital. The ending is the same as the last two; there are no additional episodes.

The 1950s provided an opportunity for Mae to enjoy the fruits of her labor, and in early January 1952, rare accounts show that she stayed at the Shore Club in Miami, Florida. Records were not maintained that far back, and it is not known how long she vacationed there. The Shore Club is still in Miami but has had a few changes since then.

Rested from a well-deserved vacation, Mae and her talents were again called on in mid-1953 when CBS decided to launch the first interactive television series, *Winky Dink and You*, which first aired at 10:00 a.m. on October 10, 1953. The core of the show involved the use of a magic drawing screen that was nothing more than a clear (actually a light-green-tinted) vinyl plastic membrane that would be placed over the television screen held by static electricity. Parents were encouraged to send for one of the two types of Winky Dink kits, with the deluxe model containing the vinyl membrane, special magic crayons, and a wipe cloth. Children were encouraged to help Winky Dink out of trouble by drawing something on the television screen, with such as a line serving as a bridge to allow Winky Dink to cross a stream, or they might even draw a moustache to disguise Woofer from the Harum Scarum. Another popular use would be to decode secret messages: an image would be displayed on the television screen showing only vertical lines of the letters of the secret message that the children were asked to trace before the missing horizontal lines would be displayed. Once they were traced, the secret message would be displayed.

Hosted by Jack Barry, *Winky Dink* was called the "first interactive TV show" by Bill Gates; the show featured the adventures of a star-headed boy cartoon character Winky Dink (voiced by Mae Questel) and his dog, Woofer. The program was very successful because of its pioneering interactive marketing scheme, but the show was halted, ending on April 27, 1957, primarily because of concern over X-radiation emissions harming children who had to sit so close to the television screen. Another problem, not thought of at first, was that children who did not have a vinyl membrane to place on the screen would inevitably draw on the television screen glass with their crayons, markers, and even permanent markers, often damaging or ruining the very expensive televisions. Parents were not at all happy with this, and many complaints were received. Mae provided the voice of Winky Dink for all episodes.

The show revived in syndication in 1969 and ended in 1973; Mae was not active in that production.

In 1955, Paramount Pictures announced that they were selling their short films and cartoons. These included the Max Fleischer features *Gulliver's Travels* and *Mr. Bug Goes to Town*. (Some sources indicate that Mae performed a voice characterization for

Mr. Bug Goes to Town, but her name does not appear in the credits. Margie Hines is sometimes given credited for the voice of Mrs. Ladybug; this is un-credited in the movie). Also included in the sale were *Inkwell Imps*, Max Fleischer's Koko the Clown cartoons; *Screen Songs*, except the last six which had been sold to Harvey Comics; *Talkartoons; Betty Boop; Color Classics; Gabby's Stone Age Cartoons; Animated Antics*; and the Fleischer two-reelers *Raggedy Ann and Raggedy Andy* and the *Raven*. This also included almost all of the Noveltoons released prior to October 1950, which included three early Casper and Little Lulu cartoons produced by Famous Studios.

U.M. & M. ([U]nited Film Service, [M]TA TV and [M]inot TV) won the bid in December 1955, purchasing 1,600 shorts for $3.5 million. The Popeye cartoons were sold in April 1956 to Associated Artists Productions, which changed names over the next couple of decades. The Superman cartoons were not included in the sale.

U.M. & M. replaced the Paramount mountain logo with its own blue shield logo and removed all references to Paramount Pictures, with the only exception of the phrase "Adolph Zukor presents." It attempted to retain the opening credits and replaced the Paramount copyright line with U.M. & M. copyright line. Before all the shorts would be retitled, National Telefilm Associates purchased the complete package previously purchased by U.M. & M., in May 1956 for $4 million, and the U.M. & M. copyright notices were present on the National Telefilm Associates prints.

Mae was able to take a break from a rather busy schedule with appearances and voice characterizations in television commercials for a few more non-work-related vacations between 1955 and 1957. This included time aboard the cruise ship MV *Italia*, which departed New York on February 3, and returned on February 17, 1955. In October she spent time in Paris, France. In mid-1956, she flew to Havana, Cuba, and spent some time there before returning to Miami and then home to New York. In February of the following year, she spent time aboard the SS *Homeric* from February 8, 1957, and returned to New York on February 13, 1957.

Although Mae was able to vacation, she did continue to provide voice characterizations in the Popeye series. During the periods of her trips, there are gaps in the release dates of the cartoons she worked in. Mae also continued to provide voice characterizations for Little Audrey, although there were only four between 1954 and 1957, and spent more time providing voices for the Harveytoons series, with thirty-two during the same time frame and only three in 1958.

Walter Disney opened Disneyland in Anaheim, California, in 1955, and rock and roll entered the mainstream as individuals such as James Dean, Elvis Presley, and Marilyn Monroe became household names. This was a transition period for the entertainment industry; nothing new for a seasoned veteran like Mae Questel, and she jumped at the opportunity to perform in her first love: theater. In late 1958, Mae performed a part in *The Majority of One* by playwright Leonard Spigelgass, which opened at the Shubert Theater in New York on January 16, 1959.

"When they offered the part in *The Majority of One* on stage, I was scared stiff. I hadn't worked live for years. On opening night when I felt and heard an audience again, I knew the old show business was still for me," Mae said to *Stars and Stripes* in May 1961. "But, you know, regardless of how you slice an actress, she still comes up ham," Mae said with a smile. "I longed to act with all of me, not just with my voice in cartoons."

The play received good reviews and continued for 551 performances. The last show at the Shubert Theatre was October 17, 1959, and then moved to the Ethel Barrymore Theatre, where it ran from October 19, 1959, to June 25, 1960.

Mae Questel performed the role of Essie Rubin, a role perfect for her, as a neighbor to Bertha Jacoby, a Jewish widow. Because the play takes place in Brooklyn, Mae's Bronx accent was close to perfect. The play is about a Jewish widow (Mrs. Jacoby) whose son was lost in the Pacific campaign of World War II, and reluctantly she agrees to travel to Japan with her daughter and ambassador son-in-law. Mrs. Jacoby meets a Japanese industrialist (Koichi Asano), a widower, and they feel an attraction to one another, but they must overcome not only cultural and religious differences, but fear, anger, doubt, and frustration that also cast a shadow over the blossoming love.

It would appear that Mae was busy and had to take a short break from *The Majority of One*. In November 1959, she appeared in *Bells Are Ringing*, which revolves around a switch board operator (Ella) for a telephone answering service—Susanswerphone, which operates in a basement apartment in Brooklyn Heights. Ella is best known throughout the movie for involving herself in her clients' lives.

Mae only provides voice characters in this movie. She is first heard as a boy wanting to talk to Santa Claus as Ella pretends to be Santa Claus. Ella tells Junior to eat his spinach and to behave himself. Mae is credited with providing the voice of Olga, who wanted to talk to Jeffery (played by Dean Martin) and mentions waiting to be taken to the races. Although Mae did not make a personal appearance in this film, she did contribute what she is best known for: her voice.

Starring Dean Martin and Judy Holliday, *Bells Are Ringing* runs for 126 minutes; it premiered in Los Angeles on June 29, 1960. It would appear that Mae recorded her voice parts in New York for the Arthur Freed Productions, Inc. and MGM. Filming locations include the East Village and Manhattan, New York, and Los Angeles, California. Mae's name does not appear in the credits.

With her work in *Bells Are Ringing* completed, Mae was offered a role in a screen adaptation of *The Majority of One*. With good reviews, the play was popular enough to be noticed by Warner Brothers Studios, which retained Leonard Spigelgass to write the screen version. Casting soon began at its Burbank, California, studios in perhaps early to mid-1961. Of all characters cast, Mae was the only individual to make the transition from the play to the movie. Mae was perfect for the role; it seems almost as though the role was written just for her. Leonard Spiegelgass was born in Brooklyn, New York, on November 26, 1908, the same year as Mae: interesting?

The opening scene of the movie is set in Brooklyn with Mrs. Rubin (Mae Questel) ascending the stairs to her friend's apartment (Mrs. Jacoby) carrying an ice bucket while singing in her well-known Bronx accent. Once inside the apartment, Mrs. Rubin begins eating candy. "When it comes to candy, I got no self-control," she says. She then lights a cigarette and mentions that she has a monkey on her back. A door buzzer interrupts their conversation, announcing the arrival of Mrs. Jacoby's daughter and son-in-law, who are visiting from out of town. As they greet Mrs. Rubin, she mentions that she will be moving, because "that element is moving in," referring to those of color and Puerto Ricans. Mrs. Rubin has set the stage, per se, for the prejudicial tone of the movie.

The son-in-law quickly rebukes Mrs. Rubin on her prejudicial comment. After a few awkward moments, Mrs. Rubin thanks the son-in-law for a "very stimulating conversation," then says goodbye in her clear Bronx accent. Now with the slight tone of prejudice set, the movie continues with the son-in-law's news about his new three-year ambassadorial assignment to Japan that invoked strong memories in Mrs. Jacoby, who thinks of her lost son. The daughter and son-in-law eventually persuade Mrs. Jacoby to join them, and they depart for Tokyo. After a flight to the West Coast, they depart on board a cruise ship, where Mrs. Jacoby meets Koichi Asano, a wealthy Japanese industrialist. A new friendship emerges as certain obstacles such as prejudice are overcome.

While in Tokyo, Mrs. Jacoby and Mr. Asano spend a great deal of time together and Mr. Asano offers marriage, which Mrs. Jacoby, though honored, turns down; she returns to America. Again, we find Mrs. Rubin ascending the stairs to her friend's apartment. This time, she is carrying a sterling silver fruit bowl for the center of the dinner table, but Mrs. Jacoby has a single yellow rose in the center for a dinner for a special friend from Japan. The conversation between the two women is different from their previous conversation, and Mrs. Rubin is worried about how to act in front of the special guest. After the arrival of Mr. Asano, Mrs. Rubin appears awkward with the formalities and leaves after a rather low bow and a sayonara (good-bye), leaving the two to an intimate dinner.

Mae would have spent about three to four weeks in the Burbank area for the shooting of the picture, and Warner Brothers released the picture on December 27, 1961, in Los Angeles and on January 11, 1962, in New York, to good reviews. Mae finally got her wish and began acting again, after thirty years of being heard and not seen. "So what? They paid me a fortune for not being myself."

She later shared her views about one of her lines in the movie, "I'm moving out of Brooklyn, after all, look what's coming in, Puerto Ricans, Irish, colored," saying that "The words just stuck in my craw, no, it made no difference, it was the character talking, not me, I hated to say it. Every matinee, every Saturday and Wednesday, the women in the audience would go 'ah' when I said those lines, and I didn't want it. I didn't want to be hated."

The close of the 1950s saw the end of one era and the dawn of another with events such the Soviets' launch of the first satellite, *Sputnik*, in 1957, beginning the "space race," and the first nuclear power plant in the United States going online to produce power for a growing nation. The Bay of Pigs invasion in 1961 and the Cuban Missile crisis only exacerbated the already stressed relations between the United States and USSR and the same year, nine hundred military advisors entered Vietnam, landing in Saigon.

Tastes in animated cartoons also reflected the change in times. In late 1959, *Rocky and Bullwinkle* premiered. The series followed the adventures of a moose, Bullwinkle, and a flying squirrel, Rocky, against their main adversaries in most of their adventures, the Russian-like spies Boris Badenov and Natasha Fatale. This period saw the death of many old cartoons and the birth of many new cartoons, including *The Flintstones*, which first aired on September 30, 1960; *Mister Magoo*; *Yogi Bear*; and many others as they packed the airwaves entertaining a new generation of children on television. The last year of the Harveytoons series came in 1960, and Mae only voiced six before the last aired.

Although many of the cartoons that Mae voiced in the past were now in syndication, her voice continued to be heard by the new television generation of children and, yes, adults also. These new cartoons replaced those voice characters such as Mae Questel and Jack Mercer with names like June Foray, Mel Blanc, Daws Butler, and Alan Reed, who now filled televisions with voice characterizations that children of that period would recognize for many decades.

Because she did not lack funds, Mae was under no pressure to continue working at this point, but the desire to work and perform was in her blood and could not sit idle for long.

Following the success of his comedy albums, Bob Newhart hosted a short-lived variety show that first aired on October 11, 1961, and was filmed at the Ziegfeld Theatre in Manhattan, New York, for NBC. Bob opened with a monologue titled "How to Save the World from Ruination" and performed various sketches. Hoping to benefit from her popularity, he scheduled Mae Questel as one of his guests; she appeared as herself. Although I was able to reach Mr. Newhart, he was unable to share any information that far back about working with Mae.

It was not long before Mae was once again in sunny California. This time she was to make a guest appearance on a popular television series *77 Sunset Strip*, starring Efrem Zimbalist Jr., in a Warner Brothers production about two wisecracking, womanizing private detectives who worked out of an office at 77 Sunset Strip in Los Angeles, California. The series ran from 1958 to 1964 and was filmed at the Warner Brothers Studios in Burbank, California. Mae appeared as Cuddles McGee in season 4, episode 12, "Penthouse on Skid Row," which aired on January 19, 1962. The two detectives assisted the new owners of an old mansion who were being framed for various crimes or assaulted by someone. Warnerarchive.com indicates the episode as 12 and not 18, which is sometimes referenced with Mae. This appears to be the only episode of the series in which she appeared.

Mae remained busy and soon after appeared in another series, *Naked City*, a police drama that ran from 1958 to 1963 on the ABC Television Network and was inspired by the 1948 movie of the same name. Many scenes throughout the series were filmed in the South Bronx, Manhattan, and Greenwich Village. Mae appeared in season 3, episode 20, "To Walk like a Lion," which aired on February 28, 1962, as Annette Faber. In this episode, a meek man confesses to embezzling money from his employer to pay for his mother's health care; he runs into difficulty when he offers to repay the money from his employer, who wants him embezzle more but for him. This episode was filmed at the Biograph Studios in the Bronx and allowed Mae to remain at home. She later mentioned, "I was out in California for a while, and I had a good television career going. But, I couldn't stand California—the sun, the sun, the sun, the sun, nothing but the miserable sun!"

Well, Mae had to remain in the "miserable sun" for a while longer because Paramount had another role for her with Jerry Lewis in *It's Only Money*. Filming began on October 9, 1961, at the Gulls Way Estate on the Pacific Coast Highway (the mansion scene) and at Paramount Studios in Hollywood California. Filming lasted to December 17, 1961, and the movie was released on November 12, 1962; it was produced in black-and-white.

The comedy, starring Jerry Lewis as a rather clumsy and awkward television repairman Lester March, begins with news that an electric power tycoon has died and has left a multimillion-dollar estate to his missing son; unless the missing son is found, the estate will go to his sister Cecilia Albright, played by Mae Questel.

Cecilia and the family lawyer are seen on television offering $100,000 to anyone who locates her nephew. Meanwhile, Lester has repaired a television set and delivers it to a private detective, played by Jesse White. When they watch the announcement on the television, Lester wants to served as a private eye and helps his friend get into the mansion of the deceased tycoon. When the two arrive, Cecilia goes into hysterics: when she sees Lester on the closed-circuit camera at the gate, he looks like the missing heir. It is not long before Lester comes to believe he may be the missing heir, through the help of the family nurse who also helps Cecilia. The lawyer, who is to wed Cecilia (for her money, of course), sends a rather bumbling assassin to kill Lester, but he fails. The lawyer now tries to figure out how to kill Cecilia so he will be the heir after they are wed.

As Cecilia prepares for her wedding, the assassin fails a couple more times in ways befitting a movie like this. Scenes include Cecilia working out while listening to music, and trying on her wedding gown. While shaving one day, Lester becomes convinced of who he is and quickly departs to the family mansion to inform the lawyer that he is the missing heir. On his arrival, he finds the lawyer and Cecilia dancing and rejoicing, although the lawyer is planning another attempt on Lester's life. This final attempt fails again, but this time due to the intervention of the family nurse. The closing scene shows Lester marrying the nurse.

Mae later recounted in an interview that during the dancing scene, "I'm using muscles that have been slumbering since I was a baby," referring to the fact that this is the first physical part she has had since childhood. She also mentioned that she provided six off-screen voices for the film.

Mae's time in California influenced her humor, as noted in an article dated April 24, 1962, which mentioned that Mae said that she knew of a Western star who'd been putting on so much weight lately, he'd soon be riding "wide saddle."

More work came her way in another play, *Enter Laughing*, which appeared in several different forms. It is loosely based on the life of Carl Reiner and the story takes place in 1938 in New York. A stage-struck Jewish kid, working as a delivery boy with dreams of becoming an actor, goes against the wishes of his domineering parents and eventually lands a part as a leading man in a third-rate theatrical company. In his first performance, everything that can go wrong does so—in hilarious ways.

The show was well received by audiences and critics; a *New York Times* article review mentions that "the major complaint is that it doesn't provide enough rest periods between side-splitting laughs." *Enter Laughing* opened on March 11, 1963, at the Henry Millers Theatre on West 43rd Street in New York, and among the stars was Alan Arkin. On October 14, 1963, an article from the *New Castle News* from New Castle, Pennsylvania, reported that Sylvia Sidney made a sudden exit from the play "for some official reason—'television commitments' perhaps—will be given, but spelled backwards the cast figures that means she's fed up, and they think they know with whom."

Sylvia Sidney was at the time playing the mother of Alan Arkin's character, David Kolowitz, when she left rather abruptly; Mae Questel stepped in to replace her and performed that part until the play closed on March 14, 1964.

Mae was certainly busy. Between performances standing in for Sylvia Sidney, she also opened in *Come Blow Your Horn* on September 3, 1963, at Melody Fair in North Tonawanda (near Buffalo, New York). The story is of a New York family headed by a father and mother with strong country beliefs as to how grown-up sons should behave. These beliefs are not shared by the older of the two boys, who is more interested in New York high life than he is in the family fruit business. This is cause for alarm when the younger son emulates his older brother. The *New York Times* mentions that it is not the original situation, but "it's mighty fine material for a good comedy."

This particular version of the popular play starred Frank Aletter, Mae Questel, and Al Lewis (perhaps best remembered as Grandpa on the *Munsters* and as Officer Leo Schnauser on *Car 54 Where Are You?*). A single article from the *Tonawanda News* gives the only known mention of this play performance that became a film the same year by Essex Productions and Paramount Pictures and starred Frank Sinatra and included Dean Martin and Norman Lear among the long list of cast. Although the movie was filmed in Manhattan, New York, I have found no mention of Mae being involved in the production.

Mae did not get to rest long and soon began rehearsing a part in *Bajour*, which opened at the Shubert Theater on 44th Street in New York in November 1964, and played there until May 8, 1964, before moving to the Lunt-Fontanne Theater on 46th Street in New York, opening there on May 10, 1965.

Bajour is a musical comedy in two acts with twenty-two scenes, is based on the short stories *The Gypsy Woman* and *The King of the Gypsies* by Joseph Mitchell. The word *bajour* is, to gypsies, the highest of all arts, a confidence game in which they swindle lonely and unhappy women out of their life savings. Among gypsies, a talented Bajour woman is the most precious possession of her husband's tribe.

Act 1 opens with the king of the Dembeschti tribe renting a run-down store in a New York slum; then he unloads the entire Dembeschti tribe from a converted hearse. Women wearing gold coin necklaces and garnished silk-shirt wearing men quickly set up and transform the store. Soon the local police are aware of the petty crimes now occurring, and a police lieutenant realizes that his old friend, the king of the Dembeschti tribe, is behind these crimes. The lieutenant's task is further complicated by Emily, a young PhD candidate in anthropology and a distant relative of a high-ranking police official who wants to study gypsy tribes; the lieutenant feels that the Dembeschti tribe is probably the safest.

Dembo, the king of the Dembeschti tribe, soon confronts the Moyva king of Newark. Dembo wants to buy a wife from him for his son. Soon, both tribes try to outdo each other in various feats of agility. Emily finds herself immersed in the folkways of the gypsies; her purse is stolen, her shoes disappear, and she is conned out of ten dollars.

The king of Newark's daughter Anyanka resents being sold, and the king of the Dembeschti's son Steve dislikes the proposal also, but soon insults turn to embraces. Anyanka reveals that her father has tried to sell her to other tribes before and kept the down payment after they were unable to pay for her. But this time she will outsmart her father and raise the money to buy herself. But to pull off a big bajour, "now all we need is some dame with life savings. A sweet, silly, middle-aged woman with . . ." Enter Mrs. Helene Kirsten (played by Mae Questel), Emily's mother, who is looking for her daughter and soon discloses the loneliness of her widowhood; even $75,000 worth of her husband's insurance would make her life better.

Momma (Mae) returns to the *ofisa* (fortune-teller parlor) and becomes more involved in the swindle as Anyanka convinces her that the insurance money has a curse placed on it by her late husband and that if she brings her $10,000, Anyanka will remove the evil spell. After Momma leaves, all burst into song and dance celebrating the big bajour.

Act 2 begins with Momma on the telephone leaving word for Dembo to inform Anyanka not to worry about the money because she has decided to give it to the Gray Ladies Guild at a fund-raiser. Anyanka tricks Emily to take her to the fund-raiser, and just as Momma is about to pledge her money, the Dembeschti crash the party and take Momma to the ofisa, where Anyanka convinces her that she almost passed the evil curse to the Gray Ladies. Momma is told that to break the curse, she must bring the money to the ofisa in small bills so the curse can be broken into little pieces.

When Emily tells Momma that gypsies often swindle women, Momma insists that they have not asked for money and, a good Jewish mother, reminds Emily that she is still unmarried and that life has to be taken on faith and offers no guarantees. At the ofisa, now decorated as an Egyptian temple, Anyanka presents herself with an air of authority. When Momma puts the money in a purse, Anyanka begins a mysterious incantation and enters into a trancelike state, swaps the purse with a decoy, and sends Momma off with a word of caution not to open the purse for seven days or the money will change to blank paper. The bajour has succeeded.

When the police lieutenant and Emily enter the now-empty store, the lieutenant starts to explain that the swindle is just part of gypsy life. The king of Newark bursts in, upset because his daughter has pulled a bajour on him and has given him a purse filled with blank paper also.

Of the sixteen musical numbers performed during the play, Mae had a solo in act 2, number 6, and performed with Chita Rivera (Anyanka) and with a woman's ensemble. In act 2, both scene 2 and 7 take place in Momma's kitchen. After 218 performances (this number varies from article to article), the play closed on June 12, 1965, while at the Lunt–Fontanne Theatre.

Mae saw the United States enter into another conflict in 1965 with the beginning of the war in Vietnam. About 3,500 US Marines arrived in Da Nang, becoming the first US ground troops there. Racial tensions increased as civil rights marchers voiced their opinions on many fronts and the first of the war protestors marched. Entering turbulent times, the nation would change.

Meanwhile, Helen Kane had been battling breast cancer for almost a decade. She died September 26, 1966, at the age of sixty-six, in her apartment in Jackson Heights, Queens (New York), with Daniel Healy, her husband of twenty-seven years, at her bedside. Helen was buried at the Long Island National Cemetery, East Farmingdale, Suffolk County, New York.

CHAPTER 4. 1967–1998

In early 1967, a few newspapers announced that Mae had returned to Hollywood to begin work in the movie *Funny Girl*. Filming began at stage 4 at the Columbia/Sunset Gower Studios in Hollywood and released on September 19, 1968. Mae worked with notable actors such as Barbra Streisand, Omar Sharif, and Walter Pidgeon just to name a few.

The opening scene finds Barbra Streisand as Fanny sitting in an empty theater looking at an empty stage. The next scene Mae Questel, playing Mrs. Strakosh, is sitting at a table with three older women playing poker; then she sings a short song before Fanny's mother sings a short song, and the scene finishes with Mrs. Strakosh singing another short song. Fanny later tries out for a part as a chorus girl but is fired. She does not give up and tries out for a part roller skating in a chorus line, but that does not work out either. But she discovers that she is able to sing and is a hit with the audience, which lands her a prestigious position as a Ziegfeld girl. There are several scenes of the audience with Mrs. Strakosh in the center watching the Ziegfeld follies.

Backstage Mr. Ziegfeld (played by Walter Pidgeon) is talk-ing with Fanny and her mother, and Mrs. Strakosh congratu-lates her and then is introduced to Mr. Ziegfeld. Mrs. Strakosh tells him that he is a genius for staging Fanny the way he did.

At the tavern that Fanny's mother owns, Mrs. Strakosh dances with Mr. Arnstein (played by Omar Sharif) and asks him if he's married; then the scene changes as Fanny asks him what he does, and he replies that he lives and gambles. The scene changes as Mrs. Strakosh asks him if she could "interest him in a friendly game of poker, three cents limit." Mr. Arnstein, Mrs. Strakosh, and two other ladies sit at a table and begin the game. Mr. Arnstein turns to see Mrs. Strakosh trying to peek at his hand as he discovers that he is holding four aces and a king. Mrs. Strakosh again tries to peek at his hand, and he folds, telling the ladies that they are too good for him. Mrs. Strakosh wins the hand with two pair and collects her chips. Mrs. Strakosh then expresses her happiness to Fanny as she approaches the table and tells her that only one thing would make her happier—and that is to dance at her wedding. She tells Fanny this as she is looking at Mr. Arnstein. As Fanny turns to walk away, Mrs. Strakosh grabs her and forces her to sit next to Mr. Arnstein and tells them to talk. Mrs. Strakosh is acting more like a typical Jewish mother in that scene than a friend of the family.

As the movie moves along, Fanny and Mr. Arnstein explore their growing feelings for one another, but busy lives keep them apart. A year passes when they meet again while in Baltimore on tour. After a very intimate period in Mr. Arnstein's room, they dine together. The scene switches to Mrs. Strakosh, Fanny's mother and two other women playing poker, and Mrs. Strakosh wins a hand as they all discuss Fanny.

Fanny leaves the follies in Baltimore to go to New York to join Mr. Arnstein on a ship, and he proposes to her. After he wins a great deal of money at a poker game, they are married. Soon after, they move into a mansion and have a baby girl. But his oil deal falls through, and they have to sell the mansion as he continues to have a run of bad luck; and as his bad financial problems continue, Fanny's fame increases. Trying to make some needed money, he gets involved in an illegal activity, is caught, and pleads guilty to the charge in court. Feeling very bad for himself, he tells her they should divorce because he feels he is not worthy of her. Fanny tries to continue with her life in the theater as he leaves for prison for eighteen months. After his release, they try to start where they first met, but he is unable to go on; and leaves. Fanny gives her final performance, singing that she will always be his.

The film was nominated for eight Oscars, including categories of best picture and best cinematography, but won only one award; best actress went to Barbra Streisand. In 1975, Streisand starred in a sequel, *Funny Lady*, alongside James Caan and received reviews such as "a far less distinguished musical which badly lacked the bravura sparkle and emotional depth of the original."

Mae later shared in an interview about a scene that director William Wyler "had me do over 18 times." She added that finally she approached him and said, "Mr. Wyler, what am I doing that's wrong?" He looked at her and said, "Nothing. When I get exactly what I want, then I will print it." She said that she watched Barbra Streisand do a take thirty-three times for Wyler without even a murmur from Miss Streisand.

I encountered a single reference source that referred to "Mae Questel Day in Indianapolis," and that a special day was set aside to honor her, but that was not completely true. The *Indianapolis Star* featured an article on October 18, 1968, "Neighbor of 'Funny Girl' Is Here." Mae was in Indianapolis to promote a two-day premiere of *Funny Girl* at the new Eastwood Theatre. This appearance included entertaining a large gathering at the Indianapolis Press Club on October 17 with many tales of her life on what formerly was called the "wicked Stage." The Press Club was sponsoring the presentation of *Funny Girl* for the benefit of its Maurice Early Scholarship fund.

Mae took time out during lunch while at Indianapolis Press Club to entertain several children with her voices of Betty Boop, Olive Oyl, Popeye, Little Lulu, Little Audrey, and Casper the Friendly Ghost. "There's too much violence in today's cartoons," Mae mentioned after entertaining the children. "There is no one for little girls to identify with." Mae shared that she is now entertaining her granddaughter Melissa, daughter of Robert, who was four at the time of the interview.

"I'm hoping Betty Boop will appeal to little girls," Mae continued. "This kind of cartoon is easy to watch, no slam-bang stuff, no violence; we need a new female image in today's cartoons." Mae's vision would come true in a couple years.

Taking a break from movies, Mae returned to her first love, Broadway, and performed in *A Barrel Full of Pennies* first presented at the Playhouse on the Mall, in Paramus, New Jersey, on May 12, 1970. An actual copy of the full script was available for review, and Mae is mentioned in the credits as playing the role of Mina, the mother. The two-act play takes place in the home of Adonis Samaritan.

The story: In the household of Adonis Samaritan, cab driver and lover of humankind, all homeless creatures, dogs, lame ducks, and people—are welcome, much to the distress of daughter Alicia, who wishes she didn't have to be embarrassed at the thought of inviting her elegant boyfriend, Milton, to dinner. But plans are made, only to be jeopardized by the arrival of still another "stray," a self-proclaimed folk singer named Alvin, whom Adonis brings home to join "Cousin" Lu, "Uncle" Nemo, and the assorted animals quartered in the cellar. Despite the best intentions of Adonis and his wife, Mina (played by Mae Questel), to have things go smoothly, they go, as luck would have it, quite the opposite, and the complications multiply hilariously. In the end Milton (who never does show up) is forgotten about in the turmoil while Alvin (who shows up better than expected) proves that love will find a way—and, what is more important, that the wild and wonderful lifestyle of the Samaritans has found a new champion to keep it spinning along merrily for many years to come.

Following is a description of act 1, scene 1 and "sets the stage" for the play that Mae performed in:

Place: The home of Adonis Samaritan,

Time: The present. Spring.

At Rise (curtain rise): The scene is of the downstairs living room in an old frame house built around the turn the century and furnished with limited taste and obviously a limited bank account. The entrance is Stage Right opening onto a porch. Beside the door is a large wood barrel. Upstage Center is the stairs leading to the bedrooms. Under the stairs is a door leading treacherously down to the basement. The furniture is "Abused Early Depression." A sofa is Downstage, almost Center. The rest of the furniture in the room is obscured by wooden packing boxes that have been converted into bird cages. Wall space is also covered with hanging bird cages. Five dogs of various sizes and breeds are tied to furniture about the room. Several big red balloons, from which hang tiny toys and messages on streamers, are propped on their reeds on lamps and bookends to keep them off the floor.

As the curtain rises, we also discover Uncle Nemo, a sweet-faced, shrunken octogenarian weighing less than ninety pounds, standing facing the audience Stage Left. His sweater is a hand-me-down that reaches almost to his knees and hangs over his hands, making him look even more diminutive. He smiles shyly and so ends the opening scene.

A Barrel Full of Pennies was popular enough to be performed many times beginning in the late 1950s and has continued to be performed to present times.

Mae did not rest long. An Associated Press article announced on November 11, 1969, that Mae had signed a contract to appear in the movie *Move*, which was shot on location in New York for two-and-a-half weeks before moving to Hollywood. *Move*, starring Elliot Gould and Paula Prentiss, was released on July 31, 1970, at the Baronet Theater 59th Street at Third and the Criterion Theatre Broadway at 45th Street, New York.

The film follows a would-be playwright Hiram Jaffe (played by Elliott Gould) over a period of several days. He and his wife (played by Paula Prentiss) are trying to move to a new apartment on the west side of New York and encounters problems with the mover. Hiram supplements his income as a pornography writer by walking dogs. When he suspects that someone is stealing from the new apartment, he recruits two of the largest dogs from their owners, one of whom is Mrs. Katz (played by Mae Questel), and then visits the apartment to find no one. Stressed by various other problems, Hiram retreats into various fantasies.

Only a few cast members responded to my inquiries and did not work with or meet Mae. It appears that her role was filmed in New York, perhaps within a single day, and she did not interact with many other cast members. Although Mae's name is mentioned in the credits, her role was minor in this R-rated film that runs for ninety minutes.

Four months after the release of *Move*, the sixty-two-year-old Mae married Jack Shelby on November 19, 1970, in what appears to be a small Las Vegas wedding.

On June 25, 1972, Feature House of New York announced that it had converted one hundred black-and-white Betty Boop films to color and had packaged them for syndication to television stations. It is not clear whether Mae would receive royalties from this, or how much. An article in an Andersen, Indiana, newspaper indicated that she would.

In mid-1972, two employees of King Feature Syndicate, one of the largest merchandise licensing companies in the world, had rediscovered Popeye's first animated cartoon appearance with Betty Boop while reviewing archived film. The two employees noticed that Betty Boop had not been seen or heard for too many years, realized the possible marketing potential of this lost icon of a bygone era, and contacted the owner at the time, Richard Fleischer, and on August 1, 1972, Fleischer Studios signed a contract with King Features.

This was great news not only for Betty Boop and Mae Questel but also for Fleischer Studios. Sometime during the last week of August, Max Fleischer had fallen and injured his left leg, requiring him to be hospitalized. The leg became gangrenous despite the care he was receiving at the hospital. Richard Fleischer shared several accounts of his father's state while in the hospital. The doctor insisted on removing the leg, but he was told no, and Richard's mother would not give them permission. On September 10, Max was visited by his wife and son, and although they believed that Max was unconscious, he grabbed his wife's hand while they were standing at his bedside and would not let go. Richard mentioned that was difficult for him because he felt that his father knew that he was dying and did not want to be left alone.

Early the following morning, September 11, 1972, Max Fleischer passed away at the age of eighty-nine. Max never got to see Fleischer Studios blossom into a multimillion-dollar company—a wish of his for many years—and of the revised popularity of his creation, Betty Boop. Although a great loss to the cartoon industry and Mae lost a man who meant a great deal to her, she also got her wish, and Betty Boop would reappear and become a worldwide recognized icon.

In August 1973, Mae appeared in a short-run series: *The Corner Bar*. *The Corner Bar* followed the lives of patrons of a New York tavern Grant's Tomb. The owner of the tavern in season one was Harry Grant (played by Gabriel Dell) and in season two, Mae (played by Anne Meare) and Frank (played by Eugene Roche). The series aired on ABC and was produced by Alan King Productions. The series ran for two seasons: June 1972 to August 1973.

In the final episode, season 2, episode 6, titled "Aunt Blanche," trouble was brewing at the tavern. Mae sympathized with her aunt Blanche (played by Mae Questel), who has been down in the dumps because her husband is working the night shift. Mae and Frank decide to bring Aunt Blanche in as a cook because she is a great cook on the outside. Problems begin on the first day as she overwhelms the staff and patrons with all too often given motherly advice (a role well suited for Mae Questel, in her very familiar Bronx accent). Aunt Blanche orders Meyer the waiter to straighten up as he walks, or he'll "grow up round shouldered." She forces customers to "finish everything on the plate" and she even makes Phil the lawyer drink milk instead of martinis. Slowly and politely, the patrons begin to leave, one by one, and do not return until Aunt Blanche is gone for good. The owners devise a scheme to make her leave of her own accord, which they do without hurting anyone's feelings, and their patrons begin to return.

This series is a lot like *Cheers*, though ten years before. A short review mentioned that the producer had brought Mae Questel on for two reasons—her accent and her popularity—hoping to help the sliding ratings of the show. Unfortunately, it was not enough, and the series only ran for sixteen episodes.

Taking a break from her other obligations, Mae appeared on the *Mike Douglas Show*, season 16, episode 130, which aired on March 29, 1978. The *Mike Douglas Show* was a variety show out of Cleveland, Ohio, and then Philadelphia, Pennsylvania, and was broadcast during the daytime. The structure of the show was similar to *The Tonight Show* with Johnny Carson and the *Merv Griffin Show* and was very popular at the time.

Mae's guest appearance on the show begins with Mike Douglas and co-host Joyce DeWitt with Mae holding a roll of Scott paper towels (in reference to Mae's popular television commercial appearances) as she tells Joyce, "Better weight it yourself, honey," as she hands the roll to Joyce.

As the show is already underway when Mike introduces her, he describes her voice work as a picture of Betty Boop, Jack Mercer, in character as Popeye, and early Mae fill the screen. Mae makes an entrance, approaches the stage, and kisses Joyce and Mike as another guest, Dennis Wise, an Elvis impersonator, sits down. Mae comments that "you can't begin a show without kisses."

Mike begins by commenting on her unique voice that he would know anytime or in any part of the world. Mae comments, in character, "I don't know about that," which prompts laughter from everyone. Mike responds in a character known from her Scott paper towel commercials: "Weight it for yourself, honey." Mae then draws back into the voice character from the commercials again and replies, "I usually do," and adds, "Everyone asks where are your Scott paper towels and do you really think they're heavier, but they are!" I am sure that Scott Paper Company appreciated the product endorsement.

Mike asks if people really do ask her that, as she reaches over and attempts to wipe a lipstick smudge from his cheek. Mike then asks if it has been a financial pleasure being Aunt Bluebell. Mae composes herself before responding, "But, honey, are you making any money, that's all I want to know," in a singing voice with a certain amount of pomp as she looks right into the camera. "I'm working with lovely people," she says and reflects for a moment before adding, "Some people."

Mike asks how often she performs in commercials, and Mae responds that they do about six or seven commercials a year, which take her away to "California, Las Vegas, all the nice places for a vacation," she replies with a giggle. Mae continues, mentioning that she does other things also, as she repositions herself in the chair and turns to Mike. "I don't want you to strain yourself." This prompts laughter from the audience. Mike then comments that she has done other commercials, which prompts Mae to say, "Lots of 'em," before he mentions her work with Bromo Seltzer because they thought she was a midget. This prompts laughter from the audience. "You know, the midget Alka Seltzer," she interjects. Mike then asks if that was a voice-over, and Mae eagerly responds, "A voice-over, I started all those," and mentions that they were great because you don't have to put a girdle on. Mike responds that you don't have to strain yourself.

As Mae begins reminiscing, Mike interrupts her politely by asking about her lines for the Bromo Seltzer commercial. She slips into character, "Bubbly, Bubbly Bromo," she sings, and then mentions that she would sing a song in the commercials, which makes Mike ask what. Mae responds that she could not remember what, as it was about ten or eleven years ago. Mae continues, indicating that she really started making commercials by dubbing voices from the training she got way back when she was voicing Betty Boop cartoons and all the ad-libs she performed in those cartoons.

Mike then asks about the voices she performed in vaudeville, again preventing Mae from slightly reminiscing about the fun she had during the Betty Boop years. Mae pauses for a moment before responding that she performed comedy and sang songs by herself. Mike asks, "Stand-up comedy?" Mae replies, "No, not really," and again says that she sang and did comedy and that she was a mimic, which prompts Mike to ask, "Who did you mimic?" "Everyone, not well, but everybody." Mike then mentions that most people in this business began that way, and Mae begins to reminisce, describes a performance she did in a Betty Boop cartoon, and slips into a Marlene Dietrich impression by lowering her voice and singing a very short number that Marlene Dietrich was well known for. This prompts Mike to respond, "There's that band again," which causes everyone to laugh and applaud.

Mike waits for the audience to quiet down for a moment and then asks Mae when she did her first Betty Boop cartoon. Mae joyfully responds, "in the early thirties," as a very early picture of Mae, taken about the same time, comes up on the screen as Mae mentions that the first Betty Boop cartoon was called *Betty Co-ed* (aired August 1, 1931, and Rudy Vallee sang in that short). Mike draws Mae to the photograph on the monitor next to them.

"Isn't that adorable," Mae comments. Mike then says that she even looked like Betty Boop. "Yes, I was, I was the model," Mae responds. "They made a caricature of my face," she says before the shot switches back to the studio with Mike and Mae looking to the monitor. "Oh Mae, for crying out loud!" she says, waving her hand at the monitor before laughing. Mike continues, asking how she was chosen, and Mae responds that she was chosen because of her voice and that after a few cartoons as "Betty Co-ed," Fleischer Studios decided to use her as a model with all the spit curls, drawing small circles on her face with her fingers, and mentions that she was a little slimmer then. Mike, being a gracious host, responds, "Not a whole lot." She then begins to share with the audience how difficult it was to get into her dress and says she had to get a larger one.

Mike changes the topic by requesting that Mae do a little Betty Boop. "Why not, I rehearsed it," she answers, prompting laughter and applauding from everyone as Mike holds Mae's hand. He has her stand just in front of her chair as the band begins to play. Mae gets into the beat of the song and into character, and then she sings one of her very early songs, "Button up your Overcoat" and a healthy "boop boop a doop" is, of course, injected, which prompts applause from everyone. She continues with the song and finishes with another "boop boop a doop." Mike stands, applauding, which prompts the audience members to show their appreciation for her performance. Mae blows a kiss to everyone. "Aunt Bluebell herself," Mike says, leading into a commercial break.

Following the break, Mike begins by asking about her performance as Popeye while Jack Mercer served during World War II. Mae responds that she performed about eight or ten voice characterizations of Popeye cartoons. Mike then points at Joyce DeWitt and says, "Wait till you hear how she got the Olive Oyl voice." "Oh, that's funny, isn't it?" Mae quickly responds. "As a mimic, ZaSu Pitts" (star of many silent movies). Mae shares the first time she saw the storyboard for Olive Oyl. "I nearly fainted," she says. "Look at this face and legs and the whole bit." She reminisces for a brief moment. "I wonder who, Max Fleischer at the time, asked, what kind of voice do you ought to do?" she says before slipping into the Olive Oyl character. "Oh dear, I don't know what to do or say." This prompts applause from everyone.

Mike draws back to his question following the break about the voice of Popeye. Mae explains that a voice (person) was ready at the recording studio to perform as Popeye in Jack Mercer's absence. Mae continued to explain about the experience and know-how of the man who got "mic fright" while they were at the RCA Studios. He was unable to perform, so Mae stepped in. "The engineer did a little engineering." She continues with hand gestures that a recording engineer may make by turning knobs, and slips into a voice character, "Wow, blow me down. What a girl," she says with a Bronx accent on the word *girl*. Mae began to sing a Popeye song: "Shiver me timbers, blow me down, if you ain't the purdiest girl in town." She finishes with a sound that Popeye was well known for, which prompts applause from the audience as Mike asks if the pitch was lowered a bit. Mae nods yes. Mae says, "Let's face it, it wasn't that good."

Mike then interjects, "One little voice that kills me is when . . ." He attempts a voice that Popeye would use, which prompts Mae to continue in her Popeye voice, "Wha'cha ya do," and continues with several other sounds that Popeye is well known for, most of which I am not even going to attempt to put into words. Mae mentions that they are going to make some new ones (Popeye cartoons) and that "kids will eat 'em up, I know, kids love these cartoons." Mike then introduces his next act, The Manhattans, as he attempts to stay on schedule. His interview with Mae lasts a little more than nine minutes, and it reminds me of what Mae once said: "But, you know, regardless of how you slice an actress, she still comes up ham."

In November 1979, Mae was given an Annie Award. The Annie Award was named in honor of animator Winsor McCay, best known as a prolific artist and pioneer in the art of comic strips and animation. This award is regarded as one of the highest honors given to an individual in the animation industry in recognition for career contributions to the art of animation. Other winners of the award from 1979 are Clyde Geronomi, Bill Melendez, and Otto Messmer. At my request, a representative of the International Animated Film Society searched their archives for additional information but indicated that the Annie's were quite different from today's awards, and no video records and any documents were available for this book.

Now a true veteran of radio, theater, and television and having worked with pioneers of animation, Mae again found herself working with something new: video games. In 1982, the seventy-two-year-old Mae provided voice characterizations for a video game Popeye, sublicensed to Atari Inc. by Nintendo. This was a video arcade console game (67 inches high, 24 inches wide, 27 inches deep, and weighing 205 pounds) in an upright/standard or cocktail (flat like a table) version for two players and was coin operated. A source indicated that the game was released to coincide with the 1980 *Popeye* movie, starring Robin Williams.

Mae provided voices for Olive Oyl and Sweet Pea in the game. The voices (stored digitally) were either short phrases or single words that were keyed by reactions to what was happening during the game often as a result of an action by the user.

The outline of the game is as follows: the first challenge for Popeye is to catch hearts that Olive Oyl drops from her platform at the top of the screen. Popeye must catch enough hearts to fill up the squares on the side of his house. Olive Oyl (voiced by Mae) would say things like "Popeye, sweetheart, catch my kisses," or if Popeye would miss, Olive Oyl would shake a scolding finger and say, "You stupid ninny!" While Popeye is busy trying to catch the hearts, he must also avoid Brutus and the old sea hag. Brutus tries to prevent Popeye from catching the hearts by punching him, knocking him into the water, or throwing bottles at him. The old sea hag also throws bottles. Olive orders Popeye to "smack her smush." "I cannots do it," Popeye says, "I yam a gen'leman! I does not hit dames." Popeye can fight back by punching the bottles. When he can, Popeye grabs a can of spinach. As he does this, he turns pink, and the Popeye theme song begins. As long as the song plays, Popeye can punch Brutus.

The second challenge for Popeye is to catch musical notes that fall from a flute that Olive is playing. There is a blank musical phrase at the top of the screen, which is filled in as Popeye catches the notes. As soon as the musical phrase is complete, Popeye can move on to his third challenge. The third challenge finds Popeye and Olive on a sailing vessel. Olive is being held prisoner at the top and she cries, "Help." As the word leaves her lips, the letters drop to the lower decks, where Popeye is waiting to catch them. Joining the fray on the sailing vessel is a vulture that swoops down on Popeye, knocking him into the water. Popeye can punch the vulture, but he has to very quickly, especially since Brutus and the old sea hag are still throwing bottles at him.

Released shortly after the arcade game was a thirty-second television commercial promoting the new video tabletop arcade-style game. The commercial opens as Popeye and Brutus are fighting over whose turn it is to play the game: "This new Popeye video game has the boys fighting worse than ever," Olive (voiced by Mae) says as she enters the screen. Popeye wins, sits down at the table, and begins playing the game as Olive describes the game, which is the same as the arcade game with three screens.

This appears to be the only video/arcade game that Mae provided voice characterizations for. There was no Betty Boop video game released until 2007—Double Shift—where players help Betty with daily tasks of running her own restaurant. Mae had a brief appearance on the long-running soap opera *All My Children*, portraying Miss Hardy, that aired October 27, 1983. This is the only episode that she appeared in and her name does appear in the closing credits. Mae later commented in comparison to her work in cartoons, movies, commercials, and vaudeville: "They're all easy compared with doing soaps. There's nothing harder than doing a soap, there's no ad-libbing in a soap opera. And you tackle many more pages of script a day than in a movie."

In perhaps mid- to late 1984, Mae signed a contract and filming began for a teen comedy *Hot Resort*, in which a group of students working at a posh hotel at the Royal St. Kitts struggle to win at a rowing contest over a group of snooty guests for a television commercial. Meanwhile, the stereotypical 1980s teenagers try to meet women, and this includes plenty of nudity as they encounter women with basically the same thing on their minds. This was certainly a work/vacation for Mae as filming took place at the Royal St. Kitts Hotel in the tourist region of Frigate Bay, St. Kitts, in the West Indies.

The movie opens to find Mrs. Labowitz (played by Mae Questel) and Mr. Labowitz (played by Charles Mayer) as they check in at the reception desk. Mrs. Labowitz asks if the flowers in the room are fresh. After the clerk responds, he comments on her nice dress and asks if it is from Sears; she responds "No, J.C. Penney." The movie continues with sex-starved students in most of the scenes as they try to meet women also staying at the hotel.

Next, Mr. and Mrs. Labowitz are in the dining area waiting for their food as Mrs. Labowitz certainly vocalizes her impatience about not being served. As other events unfold at the hotel, which certainly include sexual situations and nudity, the movie switches to Mr. and Mrs. Labowitz leaving their hotel room as a woman walks into her room just behind Mrs. Labowitz. Mr. Labowitz ducks into the woman's room, and Mrs. Labowitz hears what is going on, turns, and runs into the woman's room, and next, we see the woman and Mr. Labowitz being thrown out of the room and onto the lawn.

In the closing scenes of the movie, Mr. Labowitz buys his wife a present and gives it to her. She finds a nightgown, and he tells her to put it on. When she comes out of the bathroom, she turns to show a target on her back, and he is sitting at a table with a machine gun set up. The screen turns black as the sound of the machine gun goes off.

Although Mae is part of this film, if all the sections of her were removed, it would not affect the movie at all. Mae later commented, "I was in a porno movie, and I didn't know it until afterwards," most likely when the film had just been completed and had been previewed by the cast and crew. Judging by the responses from a couple cast members who did not work with her, her parts were most likely filmed separately from the others, and she did not know.

Shortly after her experience in a "porno movie," Mae found herself in a similar situation. Joan Rivers hosted a tribute to "honor" Heidi Abromowitz at the Caesars Palace in Las Vegas that aired on Showtime in June 1985, but Heidi was nowhere to be found. While Joan frantically searches for Heidi, she has her celebrity friends perform various skits and tributes to pass the time. (Heidi is a fictional character of Joan's loose woman ego). Some of these acts included Manis the Orangutan, Don Novello (as Father Guido Sarducci from *Saturday Night Live* fame). Others like Willie Nelson, Tony Randall, Morgan Fairchild, and Robin Leach, to name a few, contributed to the show.

As Joan opens the show, she is unable to locate the guest of honor—Heidi Abromowitz—and has everyone looking under the tables and elsewhere for her as she runs down into the audience swearing at the inconvenience. The first person she runs to is Mae Questel, wearing a light blue dress (her favorite color) and a dazzling necklace. "Mrs. Abromowitz," Joan said as she arrives at Mae's side, and Mae responds, "Yes." Joan squats next to her. "Mrs. Abromowitz, she's your daughter. Where is she?" Joan asks. Mae throws up her hands. "I don't know where she is." Joan, in a panicky voice, continues. "The tribute has already began. Where's Heidi?" Mae responds in an energetic voice, "Who knows, she could be in a million places." She continues, saying, "You know, she's a tramp," which sends everyone in the audience into hysterics.

Mae certainly did not take a break for long as she was called on to provide a voice characterization in a movie *Who Framed Roger Rabbit* for a character she knew very well: Betty Boop. Although the movie was released on June 21, 1988, in a New York City premier, which Mae would have certainly attended, the official release was the following day in the United States. Filming began in about mid-1986 in various Hollywood locations with

Mae's appearance required to provide the voice characterization for Betty Boop at the studio.

Who Framed Roger Rabbit set records. It was one of the most expensive movies ever made at the time of its release, topping the recently released *Rambo III*. The movie also broke the record for the longest end credits, of which Mae was included. Many characters from classic animation were incorporated from Disney, Looney Toons, and, yes, even Fleischer Studios' Betty Boop. Jessica Rabbit's inspiration was from a Tex Avery creation *Red Hot Riding Hood*.

Who Framed Roger Rabbit is the only film to unite Disney's Mickey Mouse and Warner Brothers Bugs Bunny. Furthermore, Disney showcased eighty-one distinct characters, and Bugs Bunny was one of nineteen Warner Brothers' characters. MGM, Paramount Pictures/Fleischer Studios, Universal Studios, 20th Century Fox, King Features Syndicate, and Al Capp's cartoons had character appearances also. Voices for these characters were provided by veterans other than Mae Questel, such as June Foray, Mel Blanc, and Lou Hirsch. Lou Hirsch was kind enough to reach out to answer my inquires to those who may have worked with Mae during the production, but he mentions that he unfortunately never had the honor of meeting her: "A great shame for me, as she had an iconic voice."

Unfortunately, contractual issues and time constraints kept characters like Popeye, Pepe le Pew, Mighty Mouse, Tom and Jerry, Casper the Friendly Ghost, and several others from being included. Several of those voices would have used Mae's voice had they been included.

Who Framed Roger Rabbit is a fantasy-comedy based on Gary K. Wolf's novel *Who Censored Roger Rabbit*. The movie is set in 1947 Hollywood where toons routinely interact with real people. It is a story of a private investigator Eddie Valiant caught in a mystery that involves Roger Rabbit, who is framed for a murder he did not commit.

Mae only worked for a short time in the studio to provide the voice for the Betty Boop part, but the scene in itself was fairly long and begins with the private detective sitting in a toon bar having just received his drink order of Scotch on the rocks. He pulls rocks, not ice, from his glass when he hears his name called. He turns to find Betty Boop, a black-and-white character when everything around her is in color. He asks, "Betty?" and the cartoon character voiced by Mae Questel responds, "Long time no see." (It would be easy to speculate about other connotations in that phrase; Betty had not been seen for a while.)

When the private investigator asks what she is doing here, Betty Boop responds, "Work's been kinda slow since cartoons went to color. I still got it Eddie, boop boop a doop!" The detective responds, "Yeah, you still got it," as the action switches to the stage as the curtain opens. The man sitting next to him begins spraying himself with cologne when the private investigator asks Betty, "What's with him?" "Mr. Acme never misses a night when Jessica performs," Betty responds. The private investigator has an odd look on his face and then asks, "Got a thing for rabbits?" he said as everyone turns to watch Jessica Rabbit appear on stage and begins to sing. Then he asks, "She's married to Roger Rabbit?" with surprise in his voice. Betty Boop, now standing next to him, responds "Yeh," in a dreamy tone of voice. "What a lucky girl," she continues, with her famous Bronx accent on the word *girl*, as she reaches over and closes the private investigator's mouth.

Eventually the private investigator solves the mystery and everything has returned to normal, or as normal as it can for such an environment, and toons again mix with real people. This movie is worth watching for anyone who enjoys animated cartoons of all eras.

Mae did not rest for too long, and only months after providing voice for Betty Boop for the first time in many years, she was cast in a role she spoke often about in interviews about working with Woody Allen in *New York Stories*.

The movie *New York Stories* was released on March 1, 1989. Starring Woody Allen, Larry David, Mae Questel, Mia Farrow, Nick Nolte, and Don Novello (who played Father Guido Sarducci on *Saturday Night Live*), it was directed by Martin Scorsese, Woody Allen, and Francis Ford Coppola.

The *New York Stories* is an anthology film consisting of three shorts with the central theme in New York City. The first is *Life Lessons*, directed by Martin Scorsese and written by Richard Price and starring Nick Nolte. The story has been described as being loosely based on the short novel *The Gambler* by Fyodor Dostoevsky. Nick Nolte plays an artist Lionel Dobie, who finds himself unable to produce anything before a gallery exhibition of his work. His problems are compounded by a woman who used to be his lover and assistant and who still lives with him in his studio, but she wants other things and even dates others, which causes Lionel to be jealous and pours his anxiety into his work. This turmoil can be seen in his work, and he realizes that he needs to be in this state of mind to fuel his art. Lionel meets an attractive young woman who is also a struggling artist at his exhibit and persuades her to become his assistant, which begins yet another cycle.

The second short is *Life without Zoë*, in which Heather McComb is a schoolgirl living in a luxury hotel who helps return a valuable piece of jewelry to an Arab princess.

The third short is *Oedipus Wrecks*, and Woody Allen plays a New York lawyer who has problems with his overly critical mother played by Mae Questel. The opening scene finds Woody Allen (Sheldon) discussing his mother with his physiatrist and tells him that he had a dream that his mother had died. Sheldon is driving the hearse with a casket in back containing his mother who begins to nag him about his driving. Then, back in the physiatrist's office Sheldon continues talking about his overly critical mother and discusses bringing his new girlfriend (played by Mia Farrow) home to meet Mother. Later, with his girlfriend, Sheldon returns home. Mother greets them at the door and tells him he looks terrible. At the dinner table, Mother continues criticizing him about things like losing his hair. The Mother shares pictures of him when he was a child and tells his girlfriend that he use to be a bed wetter. Embarrassed, Sheldon decides it is time for them to go. Mother disapproves of his girlfriend because she has three children from a previous relationship, and tells him not to get married.

Again, back in the physiatrist's office, Sheldon starts unloading about Mother, who visited him during a meeting at the law firm he works at. He greets Mother and a friend of hers after she returns from seeing *Cats* at the theater. When a man steps out to remind Sheldon they are on a tight schedule, Mother introduces him to her friend as "the man with a mistress."

Later, Sheldon's girlfriend calls Mother to invite her to lunch to meet the children and later, at the restaurant, Mother complains about everything. After lunch, they all go to a performance, and Mother complains about not wanting to be with the children. The performance is a Chinese magic show, and the magician needs a princess for his act and picks Mother. Mae is obviously quite comfortable on stage even in character as the magician puts her in a box for a sword trick. Sheldon enjoys watching the magician thrusting the swords into the box and then pulling them out. He opens the box to find it empty. Sheldon demands to know where his mother is, but no one knows. Sheldon hires a private detective; three days pass, but no one has not been able to locate her. Suddenly he feels a great weight lifted from his shoulders and shares his newfound joy with his physiatrist.

Sheldon visits the private detective and tells him that she was found—a lie, of course. Later, when Sheldon leaves a store, he walks out into the street to see what the commotion is, and as he looks up he sees a huge image of his mother in the sky over the city that asks him where he has been. Everyone on the street sees the same image as she scolds him about his girlfriend, and the people on the street interact with her.

Sheldon arrives home visibly shaken and calls in to work sick. As he and his girlfriend sit and watch a news story on the television about him and his mother, the anchorman tells everyone that he was a bed-wetter. They continue to watch as his mother in the sky over New York is asked questions from people in the street. Mother continues telling everyone about when he was ten years old.

The scene changes to Mother's head over the city next to where the World Trade Center towers used to be and tells everyone about him sucking his blanket when he was in bed. Two weeks pass as the city of New York continues to see and hear Mother over New York. He later tries to sneak out the back of where he works, but Mother sees him, and he is chased by a pack of reporters as he runs from them and his mother. In his apartment, he tries to kill himself by wetting his finger and sticking it into a light socket as his girlfriend complains about his mother calling her bad names in "Jewish."

Sheldon visits his physiatrist again who tells him that it may be time to try a clairvoyant but that he does not approve of such methods. Sheldon is soon with a woman (Jewish, of course) who performs various incantations. The following day, Sheldon is walking on the street when a few construction workers begin teasing him, and his mother tells them to stop. Three weeks pass as he continues to visit with the clairvoyant but is frustrated with no results. It is clear that they have become friends. She prepares a dinner, and he finds that he enjoyed himself. He returns home to find a note from his girlfriend telling him that she has left him.

After a short time, Sheldon introduces Mother (still in the sky) to his new fiancée. Mother instantly likes her and disappears from the sky, saying she will come down. Then she appears on his couch as a normal person. His fiancée sits, introduces herself, and asks to see pictures of Sheldon as a child, and Mother is quick to oblige.

It must be noted that at eighty-one, Mae performed without any notice of her age. I approached Mr. Allen for any recollection of his work with Mae, and he was gracious to share with me:

"I have only a faint memory of Mae Questel," Mr. Allen said. "I think I remember her coming, usually accompanied by her husband, a very nice elderly couple, I remember her as being very pleasant, easy to work with and having a great sense of humor. I recall only that my sister seeing the *New York Stories* was taken with what a strong resemblance she had to my mother while she was playing. When she did the voice in *Zelig*, she was not on camera and worked more with Dick Hyman, the music director." Mae sang the song "Chameleon Days" on the soundtrack for Mr. Allen's 1983 film *Zelig*.

As Mae had done for several decades, she did not take too long between performances and was cast in yet another memorable role in a movie that is a classic for many, at least one time a year.

Mae's final appearance came in *National Lampoon's Christmas Vacation* released December 1, 1989. Filming locations included Blondie Street, Columbia/Warner Bros. Ranch, 411 North Hollywood Way, Burbank, and Stage 21, Warner Brothers Burbank Studios, 4000 Warner Boulevard, Burbank, California. Chevy Chase played Clark Griswold and Beverly D'Angelo played his wife Ellen in this classic movie about the misadventures of the Griswold family at Christmastime. We watch as the doors are opened on the Advent calendar, and Clark worries about the arrival of his bonus check to pay for a swimming pool and the arrival of members of the family including his cousin-in-law Eddy, whose family lives in a decrepit RV.

Clark escorts his aunt Bethany (played by Mae) and his uncle Lewis (William Hickey) to the front door of the Griswold home. "Is your house on fire, Clark?" she asks because of all the lights on the outside, as Clark assists the eighty-one-year-old Mae up the steps. "Don't throw me down, Clark," she says as they arrive at the front door. "Is this the airport, Clark?" she asks as they enter the house through the front door. "Oh that was fun. I love riding in cars," she says after Uncle Lewis discloses that they got no one presents. "When did you move to Florida?" she asks as Uncle Lewis removes his hat and his toupee goes with it. "Ellen, are you still dating Clark?" she asks. Ellen answers, "Aunt Bethany, you shouldn't have done that!" She helps Aunt Bethany to remove her coat. She responds, "Oh dear, did I break wind?" As Clark is attempting to place Uncle Lewis's toupee back on his head, Uncle Lewis says "Jesus, did the room clear, hell no; you shouldn't have brought presents," he says, referring to the presents. "It's not every day that somebody moves into a new house," Aunt Bethany says as Clark is finally successful in placing the toupee on Uncle Lewis's head.

At that point, Rusty (played by Johnny Galecki) discovers that Aunt Bethany did bring presents, but a little different from what was expected. "This house is bigger than your old one," Aunt Bethany continues as Rusty takes the presents into the other room. "Is Rusty still in the navy?" Aunt Bethany asks as Ellen tries to get her to go into the room with everyone else and to say hello. "Hello everybody," Aunt Bethany says, walking into the next room; she repeats it several times as Rusty returns with one of the presents she brought and informs his parents that the package is meowing. After Clark shakes that package, he discovers that in fact Aunt Bethany has wrapped up her cat. "She wrapped her damn cat!" he exclaims.

Eventually the entire family is seated at the dinner table. (It was later shared that the scene took several days to shoot). Clark taps on a wine glass with a knife and then informs everyone that this is Aunt Bethany's eightieth Christmas and that she should lead everyone in saying grace. Aunt Bethany turns to Uncle Lewis and says, "What, dear?" He shakes his head when Clark's mother yells, "Grace!" "Grace, she passed away thirty years ago," Aunt Bethany responds. Then Uncle Lewis says, "They want you to say grace." Aunt Bethany shakes her head like she does not understand him. He makes a face, then shows his teeth, and points at his mouth: "The blessing." She appears to understand and then puts her hands together, signaling everyone at the table to prepare for the blessing.

As the family members lower their heads, Aunt Bethany begins to recite the Pledge of Allegiance, which prompts Cousin Eddie, apparently a veteran, to stand and place his hand over his heart as everyone else joins in. The family then tries to enjoy the overcooked turkey without anyone speaking. When Clark tries some of the Jell-O that Aunt Bethany brought, he asks her if her cat eats Jell-O (there is cat food sprinkled over the top of the Jell-O), and she shrugs as if she does not know, but Cousin Eddy mentions that he sure does enjoy it. After several comic episodes, including blowing up the cat and burning up the Christmas tree, the family is seen sitting in the family room. Aunt Bethany is knitting and looks up. "What's that sound?" she asks while still knitting. "Do you hear it? It is a funny squeaky sound." Uncle Lewis then comments, "You couldn't hear a dump truck driving through a nitro glycerin plant!" Just as Uncle Lewis finishes, it is discovered that there is a squirrel in the replacement tree. The squirrel jumps at Clark and runs around the house causing chaos as Aunt Bethany sits and continues to knit undisturbed.

Many other disasters occur, which include Cousin Eddy kidnapping Clark's boss and a SWAT invasion in the house, but all is resolved as the closing scene finds Uncle Lewis lighting his cigar and throwing his match down, igniting the sewer gas that Cousin Eddy dumped from the RV into the storm drain in the street. The explosion launches the plastic Santa Claus into the air. As the Santa Claus flies through the air, on fire, Aunt Bethany begins to sing "and the rockets' red glare" part of "The Star-Spangled Banner." When everyone has finished singing, Aunt Bethany yells, "Play ball!" The movie ends with Clark looking into the night sky and saying, "I did it!"

In a commentary, it was revealed that Mae was supposed to sing something different than "rockets' red glare," like the "Little Town of Bethlehem," but she could not get the words right. It was also mentioned that there was an earthquake during the day that Aunt Bethany's scene was shot. Doris Roberts (played Frances) shared with me that "Mae was very sweet and quite charming. She tended to stay in character, and reminded us that she was Betty Boop." It was clear that Mae had difficulty with some of her lines, and Doris continues: "If ever anyone was unkind to her, she took it in stride with grace and style"—a true sign of a veteran of both screen and stage.

As the 1980s closed, Mae watched the world of animation change with the new decade with cartoons such as the very popular Japanese Anime, G.I. Joe series, He-Man, and, in 1991, Disney's release of *Beauty and the Beast*. But, the Flintstones, Looney

Tunes, Popeye and, of course, Betty Boop also remained popular.

Mae attended the one-hundredth birthday of Betty Boop's artist Grim Natwick in August 1990 at the Sportsman's Lodge in New York. Five hundred artists turned out to celebrate what came to be the last great meeting of the golden-age generation of animation. A photo is known of Friz Freleng, Walter Lantz, and Grim Natwick (holding a large Betty Boop doll), with Mae Questel sitting next to him. Grim Natwick died October 7, 1990, in Los Angeles, just weeks after his birthday party.

By 1995, rumors circulated that Mae had slipped into the depths of Alzheimer's disease, and she was unable to accurately answer questions about her past performances by a couple of interviewers. Mae died January 4, 1998, from complications related to Alzheimer's disease, in her home in New York. She was buried in the New Montefiore Cemetery, West Babylon, Suffolk County New York, grave marker #6352.

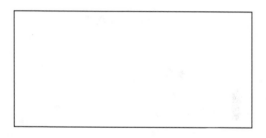

Mae's life span covered a fascinating portion of history. From a time when electricity in homes was new and many believed that "it would leak out from the wall" to the dawn of the industrial age with the production of the horseless carriage and air planes became fairly common to see in the sky. She witnessed the birth of radio and "moving pictures" and worked with a pioneer of animation—Max Fleischer—to help make Betty Boop, Olive Oyl, and Popeye household names.

Mae saw the invention of the television and how it revolutionized the way we are entertained. She saw the beginning of the space race as satellites, and later humans, were orbiting our planet and man-made crafts that explored the far reaches of our solar system. Mae lived through World War I, World War II, the Korean War, Vietnam War, and the Persian Gulf War and saw the results of two atomic bombs dropped in Japan. She saw the dawn of personal computers, cell phones, the fall of the Berlin Wall, the collapse of the Soviet Union, sixteen presidents, and four new states accepted into the United States.

Although the woman is no longer with us, her voice and images will last for many generations and will continue to entertain us as I am sure that would please her. She had once said, "But, you know, regardless of how you slice an actress, she still comes up ham"

APPENDIX 1. RADIO PROGRAMS

In November 1936, Mae began working on the *Jack Pearl Show* (radio) carried by the Blue Network. Jack Pearl played a character commonly known as Baron Munchhausen though a short lived show with only twenty-eight episodes. Mae appeared in the first nine shows with the first airing November 23, 1936, and the last November 18, 1937. Basically, Mae supported Jack Pearl's character, which was based on the fictional accounts of Baron von Munchausen, an officer in the eighteenth-century German cavalry. The show was set up in a vaudeville style with a straight man (or woman, as Mae Questel) feeding setup lines and Jack (the baron) punching them with witty comebacks.

1936

"World Wide Information Bureau" (November 23, 1936) (29:57) Mae played the baron's secretary Susie and told jokes.

"Six-Day Bicycle Race" (November 30, 1936) (29:43) Mae played the baron's secretary and told a few jokes and asked several riddles to the baron.

"Fur Coat" (December 7, 1936) (29:57) Jack and Mae played Adam and Eve in a sketch from the Garden of Eden.

"Letters to Santa Claus" (December 14, 1936) (29:47) Mae played the baron's secretary, who told a few jokes and a weather report, which included a pitch for their sponsors.

"There Really Is a Santa Claus" (December 21, 1936) (29:39) Mae answered the phone for the worldwide information bureau and played in a couple other sketches.

"Animal Doctor" (December 28, 1936) (29:46) Mae played as Susie and told a few jokes.

1937

"Doing Fifth Avenue" (January 4, 1937) (29:43) Mae played a short sketch using an Olive Oyl-like voice and told a joke to the baron.

"Badly Trained Dog" (January 11, 1937) (29:41) Mae told a couple of jokes to the baron.

"On the Way to Atlantic City" (January 18, 1937) (29:45) Mae played a waitress using a Mae West voice, and a "crazy Alice" who asks the baron for an autograph.

I spent a great deal of time contemplating how to prepare the following list. This list haunted me every time I thought I was close to completing this biography. A single source had mentioned that Mae was a guest on these radio programs, but it would be hard to invest the time required to review each show to verify whether the source was correct—in order to produce a very short inclusion in this biography. I fell victim to bad sources and citations based on newspaper articles too often; the same sources often encountered in some of these single references.

Of the following six radio programs, *The Old Time Radio Catalog* has produced most of the shows for compact disk, https://www. otrcat.com (a wonderful site for old-time radio program enthusiasts). Although these are not complete, they represent a total of 315 hours of recordings, and again, she may not even be in the series reviewed. I apologize for not devoting the time to review each of these recordings for the possibility of hearing her in an episode. Her talent as a mimic outside her own voice would only increase the difficulty of hearing her in these, if she did appear, and I can only hope that readers will understand.

1. *The Green Hornet*. American National Biography refer-ence. Single source. *The Green Hornet* premiered on January 31, 1936, and was carried by various networks and sponsors until 1953. A single reference estimates about one thousand episodes in all were produced for radio as each episode was marked by Nikolai Rimsky-Korsakov's orchestral interlude "Flight of the Bumblebee." The series is often regarded as one of radio's best-known and most distinctive juvenile ad-venture shows.

2. *Minnesota School of Air*. (Referenced as *School of Air*) *Min-nesota School of Air* was another of the many radio shows in the 1940s and 1950s using the media of radio to educate, with about 40 percent of broadcast time devoted to educational programs for children ranging from kindergarten to grade 12. Many different topics were discussed, and it would be fairly easy to see how Mae could fit with a voice character-ization. The radio program was also known as University of Minnesota Public Radio.

3. *Mr. and Mrs. North*. American National Biography refer-ence. Single source. *Mr. and Mrs. North* was a radio program mystery series that aired from 1942 to 1954 and was car-ried by several networks and sponsors. The main characters were not professional detectives, but ordinary people who would stumble on a murder once a week. The program was estimated to have reached about 20 million listeners. The series eventually made it to television from 1946 to 1954 and was carried by CBS and then NBC. The single reference in-dicated that it was the radio program series that Mae (pos-sibly) appeared on and that she could have been either a guest or a voice characterization.

4. *Perry Mason*. American National Biography reference. Single source. *Perry Mason* was a radio program crime series that aired from October 1943 to December 1955 on the CBS Network. The program was more action than courtroom drama with Perry Mason often at the center of the action.

The radio program was slightly modified for the transition to television and renamed *Edge of Night*. Mae (possibly) would have had a guest appearance.

5. *The Goldbergs*. American National Biography reference. Single source. If any of these radio programs had Mae as a guest, it would have been *The Goldbergs*. The show followed the life and struggles of a Jewish family living in a tenement in the Bronx and later in a suburban area. The show ran from 1929 to 1946 and, as many radio programs did during the era, made the transition to television in 1949 and ran until 1956. This show is often regarded as being the second-longest running show after *Amos and Andy*.

Although a collection of the show is available, it is not at all complete, and a notice forewarns listeners of poor-quality recording. I am sure it was a great undertaking to accumulate the collection that is available.

6. *The U.S. Steel Hour*. American National Biography reference. Single source. Properly called *The Theater Guild on the Air*, this show presented classic and contemporary plays and was broadcast live from 1943 to 1953. Sponsored by U.S. Steel, the show reached more than 10 million listeners and featured big name stars as Bette Davis, Gene Kelly, and Agnes Moorehead. Mae could have either been a guest or provided a voice characterization.

APPENDIX 2. BETTY BOOP

The following list details Mae Questel's voice contributions to Betty Boop. There are continuing debates about whether Mae provided the voice for Betty Boop cartoons prior to *Silly Scandals*, and because of that, the 1930 contributions are still debatable. This list is based on Mae's own accounts, on voice recognition studies I made in a studio, and on Library of Congress records.

1930

Dizzy Dishes (August 9, 1930) (6:10) Voices possibly include Betty Boop.

Barnacle Bill (August 31, 1930) (8:05) Voices possibly include Betty Boop, a flying bird, a gossiping cat, and a mermaid.

Bimbo in Mysterious Mose. (December 26, 1930) (6:10) Voices possibly include Betty Boop.

1931

Bimbo in Silly Scandals (May 23, 1931) (5:43) Voices include Betty Boop and Bimbo.

Bimbo's Initiation (July 24, 1931) (6:28) Voices include Betty Boop. A skeleton in a phone booth says, "Mae, I have a bone to pick with you."

Betty Co-ed (08-01-1931) (6:36) Voices include Betty Boop. Rudy Vallee sang in this short. Mae mentioned her contribution in this short during a 1978 interview on the *Mike Douglas Show*. She also mentioned that this was her first performance as Betty Boop. I am not sure that is correct based on my research and other accounts.

Bimbo's Express (August 22, 1931) (6:19) Voices include Betty Boop.

Minding the Baby (September 26, 1931) (7:08) Voices include Betty Boop, Bimbo's mother, and a cat.

Kitty from Kansas City (October 31, 1931) (7:15) Voices include Betty Boop. Rudy Vallee performs in this short.

Mask-A-Raid (November 7, 1931) (6:14) Voices include Betty Boop and two mice.

Jack and the Beanstalk (November 21, 1931) (6:55) Voices include Betty Boop.

Dizzy Red Riding Hood (December 12, 1931) (6:00) Voices include Betty Boop.

Musical Justice (December 26, 1931) (11:04) Voices include Betty Boop. Rudy Vallee and his Connecticut Yankees made an appearance. Mae Questel also made an appearance and sings "Don't Take My Boop-Boop-a-Doop Away" with Rudy Vallee. Mae kisses Rudy at the end of the short.

1932

Any Rags (January 12, 1932) (6:00) Voices include Betty Boop and a voice for an animal in a large group.

Boop-Oop-A-Doop (January 16, 1932) (8:23) Voices include Betty Boop, a fish, a baby, and a puppy.

Minnie the Moocher (February 26, 1932) (7:45) Voices include Betty Boop and a statue on a stairs post. Cab Calloway and his orchestra perform in this short.

Swim or Sink (S.O.S). (March 11, 1932) (6:47) Voices include Betty Boop, a mouse, and a child who lost their lollypop.

Crazy Town (March 25, 1932) (6:54) Voices include Betty Boop, a lady in a beauty parlor, and a hippo meowing.

Dancing Fool, The (April 8, 1932) (7:10) Voices include Betty Boop.

Oh! How I Hate to Get up in the Morning (April 22, 1932) (7:28) Voices include Betty Boop, a flame, an alarm clock, a hot water bottle, and a bell clapper. Les Reis and Artie Dunn (The Wandering Minstrels) sing Irving Berlin's immortal song.

A Hunting We Will Go (April 29, 1932) (7:13) Voices include Betty Boop.

Chess-Nuts (May 13, 1932) (6:11) Voices include Betty Boop.

Let Me Call You Sweetheart (May 20, 1932) (8:22) Voices include Betty Boop, a baby, and three chicks. Ethel Merman sings in this short.

Admission Free (June 10, 1932) (6:49) Voices include Betty Boop, a hippo woman, a rabbit, and two different mice. Mae also sings in this short.

Mother Goose Land (June 23, 1933) (6:49) Voices include Betty Boop, Little Miss Moffat, and one of the blind mice. One of the Library of Congress records.

Betty Boop Limited, The (July 1, 1932) (6:36) Voices include Betty Boop, a train whistle, a small cat, and a kangaroo.

You Try Somebody Else (July 29, 1932) (9:31) Voices include Betty Boop. Ethel Merman performs.

Rudy Vallee Melodies (August 5, 1932) Voices include Betty Boop. Singing by Rudy Vallee.

Stopping the Show (August 12, 1932) (7:50) Voices include Betty Boop, a woman christening a ship, and imitations of Fanny Brice and Maurice Chevalier. One of the Library of Congress records.

Betty Boop's Bizzy Bee (August 19, 1932) (7:05) Voices include Betty Boop.

Betty Boop, M.D. (September 2, 1932) (7:04) Voices include Betty Boop, a cat, a baby, and a character on a dollar bill.

Just a Gigolo (September 9, 1932) (8:07) Voices include Betty Boop, a dancer, a boy who paints a man a suit, several animal characters, and a cat walking along a fence. Singing by Irene Bordoni.

Betty Boop's Bamboo Isle (September 23, 1932) (8:07) The Royal Samoans perform several songs. Voices include Betty Boop and a caterpillar.

Morning, Noon, and Night (October 6, 1933) (7:32) Voices include Betty Boop. Appearance by Rubinoff and his orchestra.

Betty Boop's Ups and Downs (October 14, 1932) (6:59) Voices include Betty Boop, the planet Venus, a lady washing laundry, and an elderly woman.

Romantic Melodies (October 21, 1932) (10:42) Voices include Betty Boop. Singing by Arthur Tracy, the street singer of the air.

Betty Boop for President (November 4, 1932) (6:29) Voices include Betty Boop, a horse, and a pair of kittens.

I'll Be Glad When You're Dead, You Rascal You (November 25, 1932) (7:07) Voices include Betty Boop. Music by Louis Armstrong and his orchestra.

Betty Boop's Museum (December 16, 1932) (7:06) Voices include Betty Boop, a large woman being loaded into a bus, several small children running, a small person stealing a mummy, and a mummy.

Time on My Hands (December 23, 1932) (8:50) Voices include Betty Boop and a worm. Ethel Merman sings.

1933

Betty Boop's Ker-Choo (January 6, 1933) (6:20) Voices include Betty Boop and a car.

I Heard (January 9, 1933) (7:17) Voices include Betty Boop. Music by Don Redman and his orchestra. Included in the Library of Congress records.

Betty Boop's Crazy Inventions (January 27, 1933) (6:36) Voices include Betty Boop.

Is My Palm Read (February 17, 1933) (6:33) Voices include Betty Boop.

Betty Boop's Penthouse (March 1, 933) (6:15) Voices include Betty Boop, a cat, and a talking flower. A note: this is often included in the "banned episodes" of a general term of recent times deemed as politically incorrect, immoral, offensive, or racially incorrect.

Snow White (March 31, 1933) (7:04) Voices include Betty Boop, an old woman speaking to a mirror, and a mouse. Vocal chorus Saint James Infirmary Blues sung by Cab Calloway. One of the Library of Congress records.

Popular Melodies (April 7, 1933) (8:20) Voices include Betty Boop and children. Arthur Jarrett—America's song stylist—makes an appearance.

Betty Boop's Birthday Party (April 21, 1933) (6:41) Voices include Betty Boop, a baby, and a small cat. A note: there are fourteen candles on Betty's cake. This is sometimes mentioned by Betty Boop enthusiasts, suggesting that she was in fact only fourteen years of age in her cartoons.

Betty Boop's Big Boss (May 2, 1933) (6:20) Voices include Betty Boop.

Betty Boop's May Party (May 2, 1933) (6:25) Voices include Betty Boop.

Popeye the Sailor with Betty Boop (July 14, 1933) (7:37) Voices include Betty Boop and Olive Oyl. First appearance of Popeye by Fleischer Studios.

Due to Mae Questel's pregnancy with her first son, who arrived in August 1933, it is possible that Bonnie Poe or Margie Hines filled in with voices in the Betty Boop cartoons. It appears that Mae returned to the studio about October 1933 to resume voices in Betty Boop.

Old Man of the Mountain, The (August 4, 1933) (6:56) Voices include Betty Boop and three babies in a carriage. Cab Galloway and his orchestra perform in live action. One of the Library of Congress records that mentions Mae Questel. This must have been recorded prior to the birth of her first child and released on August 4, 1933.

Betty Boop's Halloween Party (November 3, 1933) (6:30) Voices include Betty Boop, a mouse, and a cat. A note: this is often included in the "banned episodes."

Parade of the Wooden Soldiers (December 1, 1933) (8:00) Voices include Betty Boop. Music performance by Rubinoff and his orchestra.

1934

She Wronged Him Right (January 4, 1934) (6:28) Voices include Betty Boop and a mouse.

Red Hot Mama (February 2, 1934) (6:26) Voices include Betty Boop.

Ha! Ha! Ha! (March 2, 1934) (6:28) Voices include Betty Boop. Max Fleischer has a short appearance.

Betty in Blunderland (April 6, 1934) (6:39) Voices include Betty Boop.

Betty Boop's Rise to Fame (May 18, 1934) (8:43) Voices include Betty Boop, a baby, a Fanny Brice imitation, and a Maurice Chevalier imitation. This short opens with an interview with Max Fleischer.

Betty Boop's Trial (June 15, 1934) (6:44) Voices include Betty Boop.

Betty Boop's Life Guard (July 13, 1934) (6:42) Voices include Betty Boop, a small fish, a jellyfish, a sardine, and another fish.

Poor Cinderella (August 3, 1934) (10:40) Voices include Betty Boop and several mice. Rudy Vallee sings. This is Fleischer Studio's first color cartoon.

There's Something about a Soldier (August 17, 1934) (6:37) Voices include Betty Boop and two mosquitoes.

Betty Boop's Little Pal (September 21, 1934) (6:31) Voices include Betty Boop and a small barking dog. One of Library of Congress records.

Betty Boop's Prize Show (October 19, 1934) (7:00) Voices include Betty Boop.

Keep in Style (November 16, 1934) (6:13) Voices include Betty Boop, two women taking seats and a woman backseat driver.

When My Ship Comes In (December 21, 1934) (6:29) Voices include Betty Boop, mice, a bird, bears, a squirrel, and voices in two old maids home.

1935

Baby Be Good (January 18, 1935) (7:48) Voices include Betty Boop, a baby's voice, a mischievous young boy, and a puppy.

Taking the Blame (February 15, 1935) (6:22) Voices include Betty Boop and Pudgy.

Stop That Noise (March 15, 1935) (6:08) Voices include Betty Boop.

Swat the Fly (April 19, 1935) (5:41) Voices include Betty Boop and Pudgy.

No! No! A Thousand Times No!! (May 24, 1935) (6:23) Voices include Betty Boop and a woman in a reserved box.

Little Soap and Water, A (June 21, 1935) (5:35) Voices include Betty Boop and Pudgy.

Language All My Own, A (July 17, 1935) (5:44) Voices include Betty Boop. Mae sings a song in Japanese.

Betty Boop and Grampy (August 16, 1935) (7:04) Voices include Betty Boop.

Judge for a Day (September 20, 1935) (7:33) Voices include Betty Boop.

Making Stars (October 18, 1935) (6:36) Voices include Betty Boop, a baby boy, baby Russian girl, three black babies, a Chinese baby, and quintuplets. This short is now included in the "banned cartoons."

Betty Boop with Henry the Funniest Living American (November 22, 1935) (6:36) Voices include Betty Boop, the boy Henry, and possibly a cat.

1936

Betty Boop and the Little King (January 31, 1936) (6:20) Voices include Betty Boop, a woman singing opera, and the king's wife.

Not Now (February 28, 1936) (6:24) Voices include Betty Boop and Pudgy.

Betty Boop and Little Jimmy (March 27, 1936) (5:46) Voices include Betty Boop and a small boy.

Pudgy in We Did It (April 24, 1936) (5:55) Voices include Betty Boop, Pudgy, and kittens.

Grampy in a Song a Day (May 22, 1936) (6:56) Voices include Betty Boop.

Pudgy in More Pep (June 19, 1936) (5:42) Voices include Betty Boop and Pudgy. Max Fleischer makes an appearance in this short.

Pudgy in You're Not Built That Way (July 17, 1936) (6:48) Voices include Betty Boop and Pudgy.

Pudgy in Happy You and Merry Me (August 21, 1936) (6:38) Voices include Betty Boop and possibly a mother cat and kitten.

Pudgy in Training Pigeons (September 18, 1936) (6:28) Voices include Betty Boop, Pudgy, and a pigeon.

Grampy's Indoor Outing (October 16, 1936) (6:14) Voices include Betty Boop and a small boy.

Grampy in Be Human (November 20, 1936) (6:28) Voices include Betty Boop and a chicken.

Pudgy in Making Friends (December 18, 1936) (7:02) Voices include Betty Boop and Pudgy.

Little Nobody (December 27, 1936) (6:38) Voices include Betty Boop, a snobby lady, and Pudgy.

1937

Grampy in the House Cleaning Blues (January 15, 1937) (6:10) Voices include Betty Boop.

Wiffle Piffle in Whoops! I'm a Cowboy (February 12, 1937) (6:34) Voices include Betty Boop.

Wiffle Piffle in the Hot Air Salesman (March 12, 1937) (5:42) Voices include Betty Boop and a mouse.

Pudgy Takes a Bow-Wow (April 9, 1937) (6:19) Voices include Betty Boop and Pudgy.

Pudgy Picks a Fight (May 14, 1937) (7:12) Voices include Betty Boop and Pudgy.

Grampy in the Impractical Joker (July 18, 1937) (6:16) Voices include Betty Boop.

Ding Dong Doggie (July 23, 1937) (6:36) Voices include Betty Boop and possibly a puppy.

Grampy in the Candid Candidate (August 27, 1937) (6:04) Voices include Betty Boop and two old ladies in a lamp.

Grampy in Service with a Smile (September 23, 1937) (7:16) Voices include Betty Boop.

New Deal Show, The (October 22, 1937) (6:49) Voices include Betty Boop, a chicken, a coo coo bird in a clock, two girl cats, and Scotty dogs.

Pudgy in the Foxy Hunter (November 26, 1937) (7:26) Voices include Betty Boop, Pudgy and a small boy.

Grampy in Zula Hula (December 24, 1937) Voices include Betty Boop, a native woman, and two children.

1938

Pudgy in Riding the Rails (January 18, 1938) (6:07) Voices include Betty Boop, Pudgy, and a person in a crowd.

Be up to Date (February 25, 1938) (6:00) Voices include Betty Boop and an elderly woman.

Out of the Inkwell (April 22, 1938) (5:52) Voices include Betty Boop.

Pudgy in the Swing School (May 27, 1938) (6:37) Voices include Betty Boop, Pudgy, several baby animals, a duck, kittens, and a girl dog.

Due to Mae Questel's pregnancy with her second son, who arrived in June 1938, it is possible that Bonnie Poe and Margie Hines may have filled in with Betty Boop voices as they had before. It appears that Mae returned to the studio about August or September 1938 to resume voices in Betty Boop.

Pudgy the Watchman (August 12, 1938) (7:20) Voices include Betty Boop, Pudgy, and mice.

Sally Swing (October 14, 1938) (6:46) Voices include Betty Boop and a cleaning woman. Singing by Rose Marie.

On with the New (December 2, 1938) (6:07) Voices include Betty Boop and several babies.

Pudgy in Thrills and Chills (December 23, 1938) (5:38) Voices include Betty Boop and Pudgy.

1939

Pudgy in My Friend the Monkey (January 27, 1939) (6:25) Voices include Betty Boop and Pudgy.

So Does an Automobile (March 31, 1939) (6:21) Voices include Betty Boop.

Musical Mountaineers (May 12, 1939) (6:22) Voices include Betty Boop.

Scared Crows, The (June 9, 1939) (5:45) Voices include Betty Boop and Pudgy. This appears to be the last appearance of Pudgy.

Rhythm on the Reservation (July 7, 1939) (5:59) Voices include Betty Boop, an Indian boy, and a woman playing a harp.

1998

Who Framed Roger Rabbit (1988) Cameo voice of Betty Boop.

APPENDIX 3. LITTLE AUDREY CARTOONS

Little Audrey is a cartoon character that appeared in a series of Paramount Pictures' Famous Studios cartoons from 1947 to 1958. She is often considered a variation of the comic strip character Little Lulu. Audrey first appeared in the Noveltoon's *Santa's Surprise* (December 5, 1947), where she led a multicultural group of children working to clean Santa's workshop while he was asleep.

In all, sixteen cartoons starring Audrey were produced for theatrical release, several of which were repackaged for television from the late 1950s on. Little Audrey had a brief appearance in a January 1948 Popeye cartoon *Olive Oyl for President*, but no vocals were used.

The pre-October 1950 Little Audrey cartoons were sold to television distributor U.M. & M. TV Corporation in 1956. Only two Little Audrey cartoons were syndicated with U.M. & M. titles. National Teleflex Associates (NTA) completed the refilming of the titles to the other Little Audrey cartoons that were sold to U.M. & M and eventually, full circle, back to Paramount (via parent company Viacom's Melange Pictures unit). The post-September 1950 cartoons were sold to Harvey Comics, when it acquired the rights to the character in 1959.

All sixteen cartoons were voiced by Mae Questel.

Santa's Surprise. (December 5, 1947) (8:20) Voices include Little Audrey, a Spanish girl, possibly a Hawaiian girl, and a black boy.

Butterscotch and Soda. (July 16, 1948) (7:15) Voices include Little Audrey.

The Lost Dream. (March 18, 1949) (7:31) Voices include Little Audrey, a ghostlike character (lost dream), and a girl walking out a stage door. Often labeled "banned" as a racist cartoon.

Song of the Birds. (November 18, 1949) (7:11) Voices include Little Audrey and a bird.

Tarts and Flowers. (May 26, 1950) (7:02) Voices include Little Audrey and an angel cake.

Goofy Goofy Gander. (August 18, 1950) (6:49) Voices include Little Audrey and a small bird.

Hold the Lion Please. (August 27, 1951) (6:28) Voices include Little Audrey.

Audrey the Rainmaker. (October 26, 1951) (7:26) Voices include Little Audrey.

Law and Audrey. (May 23, 1952) (6:12) Voices include Little Audrey.

The Case of the Cockeyed Canary. (December 19, 1952) (5:55) Voices include Little Audrey, an ostrich, a voice in a crowd, and a canary.

The Seapreme Court. (January 29, 1954) (6:44) Voices include Little Audrey, a fish, and a member of the jury.

Dizzy Dishes. (February 4, 1955) (5:31) Voices include Little Audrey and the mother.

Little Audrey Riding Hood. (October 14, 1955) (5:38) Voices include Little Audrey, possibly the mother and grandmother.

Fishing Tackler. (March 29, 1957) (5:22) Voices include Little Audrey.

Surf Bored. (July 17, 1958) (5:58) Voices include Little Audrey.

Dawg Gawn. (December 12, 1958) (6:12) Voices include Little Audrey.

APPENDIX 4. POPEYE THE SAILOR CARTOONS

The Popeye cartoons for which Mae provided voicing were a little more difficult to track than the Betty Boop cartoons. During the course of production in 1941, Paramount assumed control of the Fleischer studios, removing founders Max and Dave Fleischer from control of the studio and renaming the organization Famous Studios by 1942. Popeye cartoons continued production under Famous Studios following 1942's *Baby Wants a Battleship*. Mae did not provide voices in the cartoons from the arrival of her second son in June 1938 until May 1944.

The following are Popeye episodes in which Mae Questel provided voices. Her primary voice was Olive Oyl, but she also performed other voices, including Popeye when Jack Mercer served during World War II.

1933

Popeye the Sailor, a.k.a. Betty Boop: Popeye the Sailor. (July 14, 1933) (7:37) Voices include Betty Boop and Olive Oyl. It is believed that Mae performed the voices in this short and did not voice again until *I Eats My Spinach.*

Due to Mae Questel's pregnancy with her first son, who arrived in August 1933, it is possible that Bonnie Poe filled in with voices in the Popeye cartoons. It appears that Mae returned to the studio about October 1933 to resume voicing.

I Eats My Spinach. (October 17, 1933) (6:53) Voices include Olive Oyl and pos-sibly two characters pushed off a bench.

Season's Greetinks. (November 17, 1933) (5:58) Voices include Olive Oyl and a small dog pulling Bluto.

Wild Elephinks. (December 29, 1933) (6:07) Voices include Olive Oyl.

1934

Sock-A-Bye Baby. (January 19, 1934) (6:22) Voices include Sweet Pea. Olive Oyl did not appear in this short.

Man on the Flying Trapeze. (March 16, 1934) (6:45) Voices include Olive Oyl, Nana Oyl, three boys, and a cat.

Can You Take It? (April 27, 1934) (6:21) Voices include Olive Oyl.

Shoein' Hosses. (June 1, 1934) (6:26) Voices include Olive Oyl.

Strong to the Finich. (June 29, 1934) (6:59) Voices include Olive Oyl, children at a table, boy, "What more spinach?" boy caught on fence, and a boy feeding the cows.

Shiver Me Timbers. (July 27, 1934) (6:42) Voices include Olive Oyl.

A Dream Walking. (September 26, 1934) (7:34) Voices include Olive Oyl.

Axe Me Another. (September 30, 1934) (7:02) Voices include Olive Oyl.

The Two Alarm Fire. (October 26, 1934) (6:44) Voices include Olive Oyl.

The Dance Contest. (November 23, 1934) (6:43) Voices include Olive Oyl.

We Aim to Please. (December 28, 1934) (6:43) Voices include Olive Oyl.

1935

Beware of Barnacle Bill. (January 25, 1935) (6:33) Voices include Olive Oyl.

Be Kind to Aminals. (February 22, 1935) (5:37) Voices include Olive Oyl and birds.

Pleased to Meet Cha. (March 22, 1935) (6:40) Voices include Olive Oyl.

The Hyp-Nut-Tist. (April 26. 1935) (6:42) Voices include Olive Oyl.

Choose Yer Weppins. (May 31, 1935) (6:10) Voices include Olive Oyl and pos-sibly one of the throwing knifes.

For Better or Worser. (June 28, 1935) (7:48) Voices include Olive Oyl.

Dizzy Divers. (July 26, 1935) (7:42) Voices include Olive Oyl.

You Gotta Be a Football Hero. (August 31, 1935) (6:07) Voices include Olive Oyl.

King of the Mardi Gras. (September 27, 1935) (8:17) Voices include Olive Oyl.

Adventures of Popeye. (October 25, 1935) (7:55) Voices include Olive Oyl and a little boy. Partial live action, but the voice over is obvious.

The Spinach Overture. (December 7, 1935) (8:04) Voices include Olive Oyl.

1936

Vim, Vigor and Vitaliky. (January 3, 1936) (6:37) Voices include Olive Oyl and one or more of the women in the gym.

A Clean Shaven Man. (February 7, 1936) (6:07) Voices include Olive Oyl.

Brotherly Love. (March 6, 1936) (6:25) Voices include Olive Oyl.

I-Ski Love-Ski You-Ski. (April 3, 1936) (6:16) Voices include Olive Oyl.

Bridge Ahoy! (May 1, 1936) (6:51) Voices include Olive Oyl.

I Wanna Be a Lifeguard. (June 26, 1936) (6:26) Voices include Olive Oyl and one of the women sitting on a bench.

Let's Get Movin'. (July 24, 1936) (6:09) Voices include Olive Oyl.

Never Kick a Woman. (August 30, 1936) (6:31) Voices include Olive Oyl, training woman.

Little Swee' Pea. (September 25, 1936) (7:06) Voices include Olive Oyl and Swee' pea.

Hold the Wire. (October 23, 1936) (6:20) Voices include Olive Oyl.

The Spinach Roadster. (October 26, 1936) (6:19) Voices include Olive Oyl.

Popeye the Sailor Meets Sindbad the Sailor. (November 27, 1936) (16:33) Voices include Olive Oyl and possibly a couple of the monsters. This is Popeye's first color appearance.

I'm in the Army Now. (November 25, 1936) (6:10) Voices include Olive Oyl.

1937

The Paneless Window Washer. (January 22, 1937) (6:10) Voices include Olive Oyl.

Organ Grinder's Swing. (February 19, 1937) (6:24) Voices include Olive Oyl.

My Artistical Temperature. (March 19, 1937) (6:05) Voices include Olive Oyl.

Hospitaliky (April 16, 1937) (6:08) Voices include Olive Oyl.

The Twisker Pitcher. (May 21, 1937) (6:58) Voices include Olive Oyl and woman in the grandstands routing for Bluto.

Morning, Noon and NightClub. (June 18, 1937) (7:52) Voices include Olive Oyl and one of the voices in the apartment building.

Lost and Foundry. (July 16, 1937) (6:45) Voices include Olive Oyl and Swee' Pea.

I Never Changes My Altitude. (August 20, 1937) (6:00) Voices include Olive Oyl.

I Likes Babies and Infinks. (September 18, 1937) (7:03) Voices include Olive Oyl and Swee' Pea.

The Football Toucher Downer. (October 15, 1937) (6:27) Voices include Olive Oyl, Swee' Pea, and one or more voices of the children in the bleachers.

Proteck the Weakerist. (November 19, 1937) (7:39) Voices include Olive Oyl, the small dog (fluffy), and the hot dogs next to a beaten Bluto.

Popeye the Sailor Meets Ali Baba's Forty Thieves. (November 26, 1937) (17:25) Voices include Olive Oyl.

Fowl Play. (December 17, 1937) (7:08) Voices include Olive Oyl.

1938

Let's Celebrake. (January 21, 1938) (7:23) Voices include Olive Oyl and her grandmother.

Learn Polikeness. (February 18, 1938) (6:15) Voices include Olive Oyl.

The House Builder Upper. (March 18, 1938) (6:05) Voices include Olive Oyl.

Big Chief Ugh-a-Mugh-Ugh. (April 25, 1938) (7:27) Voices include Olive Oyl.

Due to Mae Questel's pregnancy with her second son, who arrived in June 1938, it is possible that Bonnie Poe or Margie Hines may have filled in with Popeye voices. It appears that Mae returned to the studio about August or September 1938 to resume voices in Popeye.

Mutiny Ain't Nice. (September 23, 1938) (6:28) Voices include Olive Oyl.

A Date to Skate. (November 18, 1938) (7:16) Voices include Olive Oyl.

1944

The Anvil Chorus Girl. (May 26, 1944) (6:57) Voices include Olive Oyl.

Spinach Packin' Popeye. (June 21, 1944) (6:57) Voices include Olive Oyl.

Puppet Love. (August 11, 1944) (7:25) Voices include Olive Oyl.

Pitchin' Woo and the Zoo. (September 9, 1944) (6:47) Voices include Olive Oyl.

She-Sick Sailors. (December 8, 1944) (6:32) Voices include Olive Oyl.

1945

Tops in the Big Top. (March 16, 1945) (6:03) Voices include Olive Oyl.

Shape Ahoy. (April 27, 1945) (6:51) Voices include Olive Oyl.

For Better or Nurse. (June 8, 1945) (7:05) Voices include Olive Oyl.

Mess Production. (August 24, 1945) (5:59) Voices include Olive Oyl.

1946

House Tricks. (March 15, 1946) (6:52) Voices include Olive Oyl.

Service with a Guile. (April 4, 1946) (6:13) Voices include Olive Oyl.

Klondike Cassanova. (May 31, 1946) (7:57) Voices include Olive Oyl.

Peep in the Deep. (June 7, 1946) (7:34) Voices include Olive Oyl.

Rocket to Mars. (August 9, 1946) (6:30) Voices include Olive Oyl.

Rodeo Romeo. (August 16, 1946) (6:53) Voices include Olive Oyl.

The Fistic Mystic. (November 29, 1946) (6:22) Voices include Olive Oyl.

Island Fling. (December 27, 1946) (6:40) Voices include Olive Oyl.

1947

Abusement Park. (April 25, 1947) (7:06) Voices include Olive Oyl.

I'll Be Skiing Ya. (June 13, 1947) (7:14) Voices include Olive Oyl.

Popeye and the Pirates. (September 12, 1947) (7:12) Voices include Olive Oyl.

The Royal Four-Flusher. (September 12, 1947) (6:53) Voices include Olive Oyl.

Wotta Knight. (October 24, 1947) (6:33) Voices include Olive Oyl.

Safari So Good. (November 7, 1947) (6:53) Voices include Olive Oyl.

All's Fair at the Fair. (December 19, 1947) (7:15) Voices include Olive Oyl.

1948

Olive Oyl for President. (January 30, 1948) (6:10) Voices include Olive Oyl and Little Audrey.

Wigwam Whoopee. (February 27, 1948) (7:10) Voices include Olive Oyl.

Pre-Hysterical Man. (March 26, 1948) (6:45) Voices include Olive Oyl.

Popeye Meets Hercules. (June 18, 1948) (6:53) Voices include Olive Oyl, Swooning Ladies.

A Wolf in Sheik's Clothing. (July 30, 1948) (7:06) Voices include Olive Oyl.

Spinach vs. Hamburgers. (August 27, 1948) (7:41) Voices include Olive Oyl.

Snow Place like Home. (September 3, 1948) (7:04) Voices include Olive Oyl.

Robin Hood-Winked. (November 12, 1948) (7:09) Voices include Olive Oyl.

Symphony in Spinach. (December 31, 1948) (6:26) Voices include Olive Oyl.

1949

Popeye's Premiere. (March 25, 1949) (10:38) Voices include Olive Oyl.

Lumberjack and Jill. (May 27, 1949) (6:24) Voices include Olive Oyl.

Hot Air Aces. (June 24, 1949) (6:32) Voices include Olive Oyl.

A Balmy Swami. (July 22, 1949) (6:48) Voices include Olive Oyl.

Tar with a Star. (August 12, 1949) (6:42) Voices include Olive Oyl.

Silly Hillbilly. (September 9, 1949) (6:21) Voices include Olive Oyl.

Barking Dogs Don't Fite. (October 28, 1949) (6:10) Voices include Olive Oyl.

1950

Beach Peach. (May 12, 1950) (6:24) Voices include Olive Oyl.

Gym Jam. (May 27, 1950) (6:15) Voices include Olive Oyl.

Jitterbug Jive. (June 23, 1950) (6:19) Voices include Olive Oyl.

Popeye makes a Movie. (August 11, 1950) (9:09) Voices include Olive Oyl.

Baby wants Spinach. (September 29, 1950) (6:43) Voices include Olive Oyl.

Quick on the Vigor. (October 6, 1950) (6:50) Voices include Olive Oyl.

The Farmer and the Belle. (December 1, 1950) (6:02) Voices include Olive Oyl.

1951

Vacation with Play. (January 19, 1951) (6:35) Voices include Olive Oyl.

Thrill of Fair. (April 20, 1951) (6:11) Voices include Olive Oyl and Sweet Pea.

Alpine for You. (May 18, 1951) (6:08) Voices include Olive Oyl.

Double-Cross-Country Race. (June 15, 1951) (7:24) Voices include Olive Oyl.

Let's Talk Spinach. (October 19, 1951) (5:52) Voices include Olive Oyl.

1952

Lunch with a Punch. (March 14, 1952) (5:38) Voices include Olive Oyl.

Swimmer Take All. (May 16, 1952) (6:50) Voices include Olive Oyl.

Shuteye Popeye. (October 3, 1952) (6:30) Voices include Olive Oyl.

Big Bad Sinbad. (December 12, 1952) (9:35) Voices include Olive Oyl.

1953

Ancient Fistory. (January 30, 1953) (6:50) Voices include Olive Oyl.

Child Sockology. (March 27, 1953) (6:25) Voices include Olive Oyl and Sweet Pea.

Popeye's Mirthday. (May 22, 1953) (6:18) Voices include Olive Oyl.

Toreadorable. (June 12, 1953) (6:25) Voices include Olive Oyl.

Fireman's Brawl. (August 21, 1953) (6:05) Voices include Olive Oyl.

Shaving Muggs. (October 9, 1953) (6:23) Voices include Olive Oyl.

1954

Floor Flusher. (January 1, 1954) (6:20) Voices include Olive Oyl.

Popeye's 20th Anniversary. (April 2, 1954) (7:31) Voices include Olive Oyl.

Taxi-Turvy. (June 4, 1954) (6:24) Voices include Olive Oyl.

Bride and Gloom. (July 2, 1954) (6:22) Voices include Olive Oyl.

Greek Mirthology. (August 13, 1954) (6:50) Voices include Olive Oyl.

Fright to the Finish. (August 27, 1954) (6:22) Voices include Olive Oyl.

Private Eye Popeye. (November 12, 1954) (6:31) Voices include Olive Oyl.

1955

Cookin' with Gags. (January 1, 1955) (6:34) Voices include Olive Oyl.

Nurse to Meet Ya. (February 11, 1955) (6:01) Voices include Olive Oyl.

Penny Antics. (March 11, 1955) (7:52) Voices include Olive Oyl.

Beaus will be Beaus. (May 20, 1955) (6:07) Voices include Olive Oyl.

Gift of Gag. (May 27, 1955) (6:00) Voices include Olive Oyl.

Car-azy Drivers. (July 22, 1955) (5:48) Voices include Olive Oyl.

Mister and Mistletoe. (September 30, 1955) (5:20) Voices include Olive Oyl.

Cops is Tops. (November 4, 1955) (6:37) Voices include Olive Oyl.

Job for a Gob. (December 9, 1955) (6:12) Voices include Olive Oyl.

1956

Hill-billing and Cooing. (January 13, 1956) (6:00) Voices include Olive Oyl.

Popeye for President. (March 30, 1956) (6:11) Voices include Olive Oyl.

Out to Punch. (June 8, 1956) (6:17) Voices include Olive Oyl.

Assault and Flattery. (June 6, 1956) (6:27) Voices include Olive Oyl.

Parlez Vous Woo. (October 12, 1956) (6:15) Voices include Olive Oyl.

I Don't Scare. (November 16, 1956) (6:11) Voices include Olive Oyl.

A Haul in One. (December 14, 1956) (6:03) Voices include Olive Oyl.

1957

Nearlyweds. (February 8, 1957) (6:18) Voices include Olive Oyl.

The Crystal Brawl. (April 5, 1957) (7:30) Voices include Olive Oyl.

Spooky Swabs. (August 9, 1957) (6:07) Voices include Olive Oyl.

1960-1961

Popeye the Sailor. Television series. Voices include Olive Oyl, Swee' Pea, and the sea hag.

APPENDIX 5. LITTLE LULU CARTOONS

Little Lulu began as a comic-strip character debuting in the *Saturday Evening Post* on February 23, 1935, and ran until 1944. The first animated short was by Famous Studios for Paramount, which replaced the Superman shorts. Twenty-six cartoon shorts were produced with Mae Questel providing not only the voice for Little Lulu but other characters also. Paramount allowed the rights of expire, and the series was replaced by the Little Audrey cartoon, with Mae retained to supply voices for those cartoons also.

1943

Eggs Don't Bounce. (December 14, 1943) (8:49). Voices include Little Lulu possibly a baby and a hen.

1944

Hullaba-Lulu. (February 25, 1944) (8:58). Voices include Little Lulu an angel's voice, and a devil.

Lulu Gets the Birdie. (March 31, 1944) (8:18). Voices include Little Lulu and a red bird.

Lulu in Hollywood. (May 19, 1944) (7:43) Voices include Little Lulu.

Lucky Lulu. (June 30, 1944) (7:31) Voices include Little Lulu.

It's Nifty to Be Thrifty. (August 18, 1944) (8:16) Voices include Little Lulu.

I'm Just Curious. (September 8, 1944) (6:59) Voices include Little Lulu.

Lulu's Indoor Outing. (September 29, 1944) (7:45) Voices include Little Lulu.

Lulu at the Zoo. (November 17, 1944) (6:56) Voices include Little Lulu.

Lulu's Birthday Party. (December 1, 1944) (6:33). Voices include Little Lulu and one of the children at the table.

1945

Magica-Lulu. (March 2, 1945) (7:41) Voices include Little Lulu.

Beau Ties. (April 20, 1945) (7:22). Voices include Little Lulu, Fifi-girl's voice, a voice in the crowd, and baby Lulu.

Daffydilly Daddy. (May 25, 1945) (7:03). Voices include Little Lulu and a black lady.

Snap Happy. (June 22, 1945) (7:21). Voices include Little Lulu and a voice in the crowd.

Man's Pest Friend. (December 7, 1945) (7:31) Voices include Little Lulu.

1946

Bargain Counter Attack. (January 11, 1946) (7:35). Voices include Little Lulu, a doll, and a baby.

Bored of Education. (March 1, 1946) (7:21). Voices include Little Lulu, Mae West–like woman, and baby Lulu.

Chick and Double Chick. (August 16, 1946) (6:35) Voices include Little Lulu.

1947

Musical-Lulu. (January 24, 1947) (7:20) Voices include Little Lulu.

A Scout with the Gout. (March 24, 1947) (6:34) Voices include Little Lulu.

Loose in a Caboose. (May 23, 1947) (7:02) Voices include Little Lulu.

Cad and Caddy. (July 18, 1947) (7:24) Voices include Little Lulu.

A Bout with a Trout. (October 30 1947) (7:21). Voices include Little Lulu, Lulu's mother, an angel's voice, and one of the letters in a classroom.

Super Lulu. (November 21, 1947) (6:54) Voices include Little Lulu.

The Baby Sitter. (December 12, 1947) (6:57). Voices include Little Lulu and a baby in a crib.

1948

The Dog Show-Off. (January 30, 1948) (6:31). Voices include Little Lulu and a boy.

APPENDIX 6. HARVEY TOONS/FAMOUS STUDIOS

Harvey Toons was a series of animated cartoons produced for television from October 1950 to March 1962 and produced by Famous Studios, which was founded as a successor company to Fleischer Studios. Mae Questel continued to voice characters under the new studio. Harvey Toons featured characters including Casper the Friendly Ghost, Little Audrey, Tommy Tortoise and Moe Hare, Baby Huey, Herman and Katnip, Buzzy the Crow, and Modern Madcaps.

Most productions had at least four different cartoons combined into one show that would try to make up a thirty-minute time slot for television. Mae's contributions were often in just one of those cartoons. Run times are approximate of the episode that Mae provided voices in. Dates are known release dates, and date categories are based on copyright dates from the cartoon.

1932

Time on my Hands. (8:50) Voices include Mermaid.

Sleepy Time Down South. (November 11) (8:47) Voices include fire alarm, lady on the phone about her house on fire, small fireman, fireman that lost his hat, one of the ladies in a window, and one of the keys on a piano. The Boswell sisters sing in this short.

1935

The Kids in the Shoe. (7:16) Voices include woman in the shoe and kids.

1936

Christmas Comes but once a Year. (8:15) Voices include orphans.

Greedy Humpty Dumpty. (7:48) Voices include Little Bo Peep.

Somewhere in Dreamland. (8:52) Voices include mother, boy, and girl.

1937

Bunny Mooning. (6:22) Paramount/Max Fleischer. Wedding of Jack and Jill Rabbit. Voices include Jill Rabbit, female elk, singing chicken, and three cats in a church pew.

1938

The Playful Polar Bears. (7:57) Voices include baby polar bear.

The Tears of an Onion. (6:56) Voices include various vegetables.

1940

The Fulla Bluff Man. (6:10) Voices include cavewoman.

1944

Gabriel Churchkitten. (8:40) Voices include Peter the Mouse.

1945

The Friendly Ghost. (8:49) Voices include Johnny.

1948

Land of the Lost. (June 7, 1949) (7:46) Voices include Isabel.

Hector's Hectic Life. (6:26) Voices include Swedish housekeeper and puppies.

The Lone Star State. (7:11) Voices include Little Bo Pee.

1949

A Haunting We Will Go. (6:53) Voices include Casper and Ghost Teacher. One of the few times that Mae performed the voice of Casper.

Marriage Wows. (6:45) Voices include Bertha Mouse and raccoon.

Snow Foolin'. (6:08) Voices include hen and mama bird.

Spring Song. (7:35) Voices include Mrs. Robin.

Toys Will Be Toys. (6:56) Voices include doll princes.

1950

Land of Lost Jewels. (June 1) (9:05) Voices include Isabel.

Casper's spree Under the Sea. (8:00) Voices include Goldie the Goldfish.

Once Upon a Rhyme. (7:09) Voices include Little Red Riding Hood, Little Miss Moffat, and the Three Blind Mice.

Quack-a-Doodle Do. (6:52) Voices include Baby Huey's mother.

Teacher's Pest. (6:53) Voices include Junior's mother and a worm.

1951

Tweet Music. (February 9) Voices include the little eagle and ostrich.

Land of Lost Watches. (May 4) (7:02) Voices include Isabel and Rosita Wristwatch.

Miners Forty-Niners. (May 4) Voices include gold digger and Clementine.

One Quack Mind. (6:01) Voices include Baby Huey's mother and hen on telephone.

Party Smarty. (6:48) Voices include Oscar and Baby Huey's mother.

Boo Hoo Baby. (7:14) Voices include babies.

Boo Scout. (6:58) Voices include Billy.

Too Boo or Not to Boo. (6:19) Voices include Lou and ladies at door.

Mice Paradise. (6:06) Voices include Herman's cousin.

1952

Cage Fright. (6:15) Voices include Alfred.

The Deep Boo Sea. (6:09) Voices include Billy.

Ghost of the Town. (5:57) Voices include baby.

Pig-a-Boo. (6:18) Voices include baby pig and mama pig.

Spunky Skunky. (6:06) Voices include Skunky.

True Boo. (6:13) Voices include Voices include Billy and Billy's mother.

1953

Huey's Ducky Daddy. (5:24) Voices include Baby Huey's mom.

Starting from Hatch. (6:34) Voices include Baby Huey's mom.

Boos and Saddles. (5:38) Voices include Billy.

By the Old Mill Scream. (6:11) Voices include Short-Tail

Frightday the 13th. (6:07) Voices include Lucky.

Little Boo-Peep. (5:32) Voices include Little Bo Peep.

Hysterical History. (6:39) Voices include Priscilla, Pocahontas, and telephone operator.

Of Mice and Men. (6:03) Voices include Louise the Mouse.

1954

Boos and Arrows. (6:24) Voices include Little Feather and baby.

Casper Genie. (6:22) Voices include Billy.

Puss 'n Boos. (6:02) Voices include kitten and woman.

Hair Today, Gone Tomorrow. (6:39) Voices include Katnip's girlfriend.

Of Mice and Menace. (6:17) Voices include Herman's nephew #1.

Oily Bird, The. (6:03) Voices include bluebirds.

1955

Poop Goes the Weasel. (6:23) Voices include Wishbone.

Git Along Li'l Duckie. (6:05) Voices include Baby Huey's mom.

Bull Fright. (6:20) Voices include Pancho.

Hide and Shriek. (5:54) Voices include Spooky, kitten, and Casper's mom.

Spooking with a Brogue. (6:01) Voices include Billy.

Bicep Built for Two. (6:40) Voices include cute kitty.

Kitty Cornered. (6:21) Voices include Cuddles.

Mousier Herman. (5:59) Voices include Herman's cousin.

1956

Swab the Duck. (6:43) Voices include duckling.

Dutch Treat. (5:45) Voices include Hans.

Ground Hog Play. (5:35) Voices include Casper, Hillary, and boys.

Line of Screammage. (6:31) Voices include Billy, neighborhood kid, and Tony's friend.

Penguin for your Thoughts. (6:29) Voices include baby penguin cries.

Hide and Peek. (5:48) Voices include Herman's cousin #3.

Mouseum. (6:21) Voices include Herman's cousin #1.

Pedro and Lorenzo. (5:39) Voices include Young Pedro.

1957

Jumping with Toy. (5:52) Voices include Baby Huey's mom.

Pest Pupil. (6:15) Voices include Baby Huey's mom.

Ghost of Honor. (5:59) Voices include telephone operator and painter.

Hooky Spooky. (5:34) Voices include Little Ghost's teacher.

Ice Scream. (6:03) Voices include Billy and older boy.

Peek a Boo. (5:38) Voices include kitten and scared boy.

Cat in the Act. (5:31) Voices include Murgatroyd.

Cock-a-Doodle-Dino. (6:25) Voices include Danny's mom.

One Funny Knight. (5:33) Voices include Princess Guinevere.

Sky Scrappers. (5:43) Voices include Herman's cousin #2.

1958

Spook and Span. (5:39) Voices include little girl.

Which is Witch? (5:49) Voices include Wendy.

You Said a Mouseful. (5:47) Voices include Chubby.

1959

Felineous Assult. (5:31) Voices include Kitnip.

Fit to be Toyed. (6:47) Voices include J.G's wife and little boy.

Owly to Bed. (5:29) Voices include Hootie the Baby Owl.

Matty's Funnies with Beany and Cecil. Television show that used many of the Harveytoons/Famous Studios cartoons.

1960

Counter Attack. (6:32) Voices include mouse.

Fine Feathered Fiend. (6:24) Voices include little Native American boy.

Monkey Doodles. (6:18) Voices include George's wife.

Planet Mouseola. (6:46) Voices include mouse.

Shootin' Stars. (5:47) Voices include little boy.

Trouble Date: (6:14) Voices include Cuddles.

1963

Sight for Squaw Eyes. (6:27) Voices include Minnie-Chacha. I must admit that the voice characterization does not sound like Mae in this short.

APPENDIX 7. TELEVISION COMMERCIALS

There is really no easy way to include Mae's work in television commercials in the main body of the book as her work spanned many years; it seemed better suited to an appendix. Some records indicating when she performed are lost, including those for Scott paper towels, now owned by Kimberly-Clark. This list cannot be complete; again, the only reliable source passed away in 1998. Before attempting to detail the television commercials that Mae performed in, an article in the *New York Times* offers a great introduction. Titled, "TV Ads Shift to Older Persons," the article (from 1975) opens by saying that what is new in the world of television commercials is older people—not elderly, but generally those over forty, or even well over forty, "with some of the wisdom of life on their brows." Furthermore, researching many of the leading New York advertising agencies has revealed that many commercials, already completed or in production at the time, have changed their format from those of the 1960s.

Ads depicting the young bride's clever perception of products as superior to her mother's now gave way, and she would learn from her elders. A major New York advertising agency mentions that those often portrayed as using the products are now promoting them as the "smart old hand." It appears that these New York agencies, which produce about seventy percent of all national TV advertising, draw from a talent pool of about twenty-five thousand performers, most of which rely on the income from commercial work between roles on and off Broadway. Many of these same agencies are unsure of the reason for the trend, and many agree that they happen by chance. One agency executive indicated that using older people in commercials as the voices of experience is realistic and makes good sense.

A great example of a hit at that time was a Maxwell House coffee commercial featuring Margaret Hamilton, best known as the wicked witch in the 1939 movie *The Wizard of Oz*. Several other examples that those from that generation would remember include Jan Miner as Madge, the manicurist in the Palmolive Liquid commercial, and Nancy Walker in the Bounty Towels commercials. Other effective salespeople include Robert Morley, Peter Sellers, and, of course, Mae Questel.

No single source provides a complete record of the commercials that Mae worked in, but that is my goal here. I must say how much I appreciate tvdays.com for its assistance in providing many of these old commercials for me to review. This list does not contain any radio commercials, although in theory Mae could have performed in some. In her own accounts, she does not mention that she did, nor have I encountered any. That is not to say that she did not; I just did not encounter any.

Scott Paper Towels. Perhaps the best known of all the commercials in which Mae appeared was for Scott Paper Towels. She appeared as a spokesperson, Aunt Bluebell, from about 1971 to 1978. A typical thirty-second spot would find a woman unable to choose between a plethora of paper towels on a shelf in a supermarket. In this case, a woman was attracted to a pretty design when Aunt Bluebell (Mae Questel) enters and tells the woman, "Why not get both? Scott Towels art and flowers collection," while tapping a roll of towels she is holding. Then she describes seven different varieties to the woman: "And Scott Towels is the heaviest roll you can buy," she says, as she places a roll on a scale with another unnamed roll; the scale quickly lowers under the additional weight of the Scott Towels. The woman now boasts about being practical. "Be more practical," Aunt Bluebell says, placing a roll in the woman's arms "Take two."

"Of course, my schtick, I would say, is a soft sell. And nobody has ever said I annoy them. Ever. My appeal? I think I appeal to people because I'm likeable. I'm an awfully nice lady. There's no bitchiness in me, well, let's face it," Mae later shared in an interview after the run of Aunt Bluebell commercials. When Mae is asked about the toilet paper guy, very popular then, she responds, "Oh, the Charmin' guy. Don't compare me to him, please." She continued. "To be a spokeswoman in a commercial, this is one of those things an actor looks forward to, you can sit back and do other things with a commercial. The kind of recognition I get from this commercial is like if I made 10 movies a year. It's very gratifying and I love it. People come up to me on the streets, in restaurants."

Mae was asked many times about using the product. "Of course, we use 'em. They give 'em to us, and give 'em to people as presents." Mae continued, sharing, "Last year we were at a Bar Mitzvah in Rochester and 100 people came in a snowstorm to see me. No criticism; once in a while somebody will say why don't you change your hat or get a new getup, I started with a very expensive dress, $70, and they copied it, to get it just the way it was, and it cost them now as much as $500 to copy that dress, but it's like a costume, they don't want to disturb the image, it's a small way of thinking."

Kimberly-Clark (acquired Scott Paper Towels in 1995) was kind enough to respond to my inquiry, but it did not retain any historical information or have access to information from the ads during that time. It is not known how many commercials Mae was a spokesperson for with this product or the precise dates the commercials ran.

Nabisco Cereals, Buffalo Bee. Described as a rootin'-tootin' cowboy bee, or cowbee, this character began representing Nabisco's wheat-honeys and rice-honeys cereal in 1954. Common to all commercials that I reviewed was at the beginning of each commercial was Buffalo Bee (voiced by Mae Questel) knocking on the television screen several times before saying, "Your undivided attention, please! Buffalo Bee's the name; I'm goin' to do some rope tricks. My lasso, please!" A lasso wraps around Buffalo Bee several times. "Thank you! First trick, a little rope twirling." Buffalo Bee twirls the rope and spins it away to reveal a bowl of cereal. "Next, I'm gonna make a rope square, a very difficult trick I might add!" Buffalo Bee makes a square out of the rope, which becomes a cereal box. "Now I'd like to rope some words," and three birds flap out from the side of the screen. "I said words, not birds!" Buffalo Bee jumps up, swooshes the birds away, and then snaps the rope in the corner of the box. The word *Nabisco* appears and Buffalo Bee does the same thing for the words *wheat* and *honeys.* "And here it is," the bee continues as he pushes the box over as the screen changes to a real box, some of whose contents are poured into a bowl in front of a young boy. "Crispy golden puffs of toasted wheat," Buffalo Bee continues, "flavored to perfection with beelicious honey. If you haven't tried 'em yet, remind Mom to get a package at the grocer's. Remind her! Beg her till she gets Nabisco wheat honeys!" Buffalo Bee exclaims before going into song: "I'm Buffalo Bee and take my advice, get Nabisco wheat honeys, also rice!"

These commercials often appeared during shows such a *Rin Tin, Sky King, The Mickey Mouse Club,* and *Howdy Doody.* There are several varieties of the commercial featuring Buffalo Bee voiced by Mae Questel. Although no records were located and Nabisco was not able to assist me, it appears that Mae provided voice characterization for Buffalo Bee in 1955 and 1956. Buffalo Bee was replaced by a less tough bee named Buddy Bee about 1965.

Fizzies beverage drink. In 1957, the Emerson Drug Company, manufacturer of Bromo Seltzer, developed a tablet that, when dropped in a glass of water, fizzed and dissolved creating a sweet effervescent drink. Fizzies eventually came in seven flavors: grape, orange, cherry, lemon-lime, strawberry, root beer, and cola. A source indicated that at one point, Fizzies outsold Kool Aid almost two to one.

A sample commercial runs like this: three children enter a kitchen, and the announcer says, "These thirsty children use to be a problem for mother, but no more. Now they make their own soft drink. It's fun. Mother buys them Fizzies, the tablet that makes an instant sparkling drink." As the announcer continues, the three children are preparing their drinks and the commercial changes to an animated tablet (tablet with a face on it). "Hey, kids, let's show the folks how easy it is!" The tablet (voiced by Mae Questel) continues. "Just drop me in a glass of water." The scene changes to the tablet plopping into a glass of water. "Weeee, I make the best tasting soft drink there is, and I come in five delicious flavors; grown-ups like me too." Mae's voice characterization continues as the tablet is fizzing in the glass of water, "And low in calories, watch me go! Look quick, bye!" The tablet is now fully dissolved as the announcer begins to describe the product further.

I was able to review a few varieties of the one-minute commercial, and basically, those using Mae as a voice characterization were about the same. The beginning and end characters (a clown, two boys dressed as cowboys) were different, but the animated tablet part was similar.

No records could be located indicating when Mae provided voice characterizations for the Fizzies tablet or how many commercials she played in. The manufacturer indicated that records were not retained that far back. A commonality was that there were only five flavors available at the time Mae performed in them and the quality of black-and-white images would place the commercials about 1957 to 1960. I was unable to locate her in any other product from the same company.

Popeye video game. Released shortly after the video arcade game was a thirty-second television commercial promoting the new video tabletop arcade game. The commercial opens with Popeye and Brutus fighting over whose turn it is to play the game.

"This new Popeye video game has the boys fighting worse than ever," Olive (voiced by Mae) says as she enters the screen. Popeye wins, sits down at the table, and begins playing the game as Olive describes the game, which is the same as the arcade game with three screens.

Speidel Watch Bands. The opening scene is a young couple and a mother figure (played by Mae Questel) sitting at a table when the young woman places a plate of food in front of mother. "Oh, you bought her a new watch," the mother says to the young woman, looking at the young man. "No, new Speidel band," the young woman responds. "That's nice," the mother says as she pats the young man's hand a couple times. These commercial spots last thirty seconds. Records are not available for the quantity of these that Mae worked in or the exact dates. The copy I reviewed was copyrighted 1980.

Hasbro. Mae provided the voice for the animated character Hasbro toys Mr. and Mrs. Potato Head. The commercial begins with two children talking. The boy asks, "Hasbro, what's new?" The animated character introduces Mr. and Mrs. Potato Head. "Mr. and Mrs. Potato Head, with their own cars and trailers, that's what's new." The spot turns to the children playing with the toys. "See Mr. Potato Head has a car and boat trailer, and there's a car and shopping trailer for his wife, Mrs. Potato Head. This is so fun to do and easy to," the voice continues as the boy picks up a real potato. "Like this," the voice says as the boy pushes an ear into a real potato. "Take any fruit or vegetable; then stick in eyes, ears, and then the mouth. You can make the funniest-looking people in the whole world. Potato Head people look different every time you make them," the voice says as a completed Mr. Potato Head is pushed across the screen in front of several different types of fruits and vegetables with the toy pieces in them. "Mr. and Mrs. Potato Head with cars and trailers comes in one and two dollar sizes." The voice ends then the young boy asks, "What else is new, Hasbro?" "A vanity case," the voice exclaims, "with toy cosmetics and beautiful accessories, and real-looking doctor and nurse kits," The voice continues as pictures of each toy is shown. These commercials last about a minute. No records could be found as to how many Mae worked in or exact dates.

Mrs. Potato Head was introduced in 1953, and soon after accessories were added. Mae would have provided voice characterizations in the later commercials from about 1962 to 1965.

Mackintosh Apples. This fifteen-second spot combined animation and real pictures with a man, a woman, and a child (voice of Mae) all singing as they pick apples: "We're gonna have a Mackintosh apple jamboree!" Then the man tosses an apple to the boy, who sings, "I always eat by gosh, a Mackintosh!" They all three continue to sing and dance: "We'll have an apple spree, hi neighbor, join our apple jamboree." The commercial ends as a real boy takes a bite out of an apple. It is in black-and-white from the mid-to late 1950s.

Cheerios Cereals. The animated commercial begins with a schoolgirl skipping and carrying some books when a character that looks like a roll of rope, jumps out from behind a tree. "Help! The ropeman's got me!" the girl (voiced by Mae) cries as she is carried away past a boy trimming some hedges. The boy drops his clippers, exclaims that it is time for Cheerios, and quickly pours a bowl. A jingle begins about his strength will grow if he eats Cheerios, and he now has large muscles as the jingle tells that he will cut down ropeman. The boy takes off after them. He cuts up ropeman into many pieces, and the girl now has a jump rope, who sings, "Big C, little O, go with Cheerios!" They both sing as the fifteen-second black-and-white commercial ends. There are a few variations of this commercial but with a different villain, such as a sponge monster, and Mae usually provided the voice of the girl.

Kellogg's Sugar Smacks. The animated commercial begins as a mother brings two boys breakfast cereal, and they jump out of their bunk beds. One of the boys dumps his brother's bowl into his, prompting the brother to ask where his is and for "a wonderful snack." The other boy (voiced by Mae) grabs a pillow and says, "Okay!" and smacks his brother on the head. "And 'cause you're me brother, I'll give ya another," he says as the mother comes in and takes the pillow from him. Mae, still in character, begins to sing a jingle very quickly to keep the commercial in time. The image changes to a bowl of Sugar Smacks as it is filled with milk. "She means honey on the outside, sugar on the inside, puffs of wheat, smackin' sweet, a taste that knocks you off your feet, Kellogg's Sugar Smacks!" This is a full-minute black-and-white commercial.

Bosco Chocolate-Flavored Syrup. This commercial begins as an announcer describes how the chocolate-flavored drink makes everything special as the syrup is poured on ice cream and cake and in milk. Then the announcer says to sing out (as a small chorus begins and Mae is in this chorus) "I love Bosco; it's rich and chocolaty, chocolate flavored Bosco is mighty good for me!" the chorus stops, and Mae continues: "Momma puts it in my milk for extra energy, Bosco gives me iron, and sunshine vitamin D" then the chorus takes over to finish the commercial. "That's the drink for me!" Black-and-white, the commercial runs for one minute.

Welch's Candy. Commercial begins as a small boy in the kitchen is holding a box of Welch's Candy and flicks a candy in his mouth. "Whatcha' doin', sis?" the boy (voiced by Mae) asks, and she replies that she is making candy. "Why?" the boy asks, and she responds that her boyfriend is here. "What's that gotta do with making candy?" he asks as he flips another candy in his mouth. All of a sudden the pots on the stove that are brewing explode, making a mess, and his sister blames it on him. "What a mess!" he says as the sister panics now that she has to start all over. "Use some Welch's Candy." He offers the box to her. "There's a smile in every bite!" The sister takes the box and the image changes to a real box of candy (a different type) "Welch's Favorites is a delicious assortment of six of the most popular chocolates, and that's why they call 'em favorites," Mae says, describing the box in her regular voice. The image switches back to the animation, and the sister asks if there are any more. "Tell him to eat slower," the boy responds (Mae is back in character now). "He's going through our week supply," he says handing her the box. "So, when's the wedding?" he asks and flips another candy in his mouth. The commercial is in black-and-white and runs for a minute.

Alka Seltzer. I reviewed many of these commercials that featured the small man/boy wearing a hat but was not able to locate one with Mae's voice. Although I covered what appear to be mid-1950s to the color versions of mid-1960s, I did not hear Mae's voice. In each of those that I reviewed, the voice was the same. This is not to say that she may have performed in some, but I was not able to hear her.

Mae most certainly performed in many other commercials in the mid- to late 1950s and into the early 1960s. These include Platex (1970–1972), Romila (1970–1972), Folger's Coffee (1970–1972), Yuban Coffee, S.O.S.(1981), and Nabisco Honey Grahams. Sometimes they are credited to her, though I have not found them. It does not mean that she did not perform in them; I just was not able to locate any. As I stated before, I am sure that this is not a complete list, but it is all that I have been able to watch for positive verification of her contributions. I can say for sure that this is the most comprehensive list of her work in commercials available.

APPENDIX 8. RECORDS (VINYL, LP)

This list is an attempt to place all known vinyl records in which Mae either was sole performer or a contributor. Of course, I am sure that this list is not complete. There is no single source for reference. Sources used are Library of Congress Sound Recording (SONIC), studio records if available, tributes, and sales of actual records.

1933 Victor. Mimi/The Girl in the Little Green Hat. #447

1935 Decca. Choc'late Soldier Man. #346

1935 Decca. On the Good Ship Lollipop/I've Got a Pain in my Sawdust. #653

1935 Decca. The Wedding of Jack and Jill. #510

1935 Decca. When I Grow Up/Animal Crackers. #680.

1936 Decca. The Music Goes 'Round and 'Round/The Broken Record. #769.

1936 Decca. You've Gotta Eat your Spinach, Baby. #832.

1936 Decca. At the Codfish Ball/The Right Somebody to Love.

1936 Decca. Medley of Songs from Shirley Temple Pictures. #876

1937 Decca. I Want You for Christmas. #1544.

1937 Decca. In Our Little Wooden Shoes/I Want You for Christmas. #2974.

1940 Decca. You'd Be Surprised/Oh Gee, Oh Gosh. #HL7122.

1945 RWA. *Atlantic Spotlight.* #7076 B2-3. Radio Broadcast.

1947 Decca. Oh! Gee, Oh! Gosh, Oh! Golly, I'm in Love. #2974

1957 Cabot Records. Official Popeye TV Album.

1958 Harmony. On the Good Ship Lollipop. #R587.

1958 Decca. Oh, My Goodness.

1959 Golden Records. Never Pick a Fight with Popeye. #1046.

1960 RCA Camden. Popeye's Favorite Stories.

1961 Golden Records. Popeye's Songs about Health, Safety, Friendship and Manners.

1962 Golden Records. *Popeye and his Friends.* #EP101.

1962 Golden Records. I'm a Little Teapot/Polly Put the Kettle On. #615.

1962 Golden Records. Little Audrey Says/Let's Go Shopping. #R-70

1964 Bajour, Original Broadway Cast.

1966 Wonderland. *Six Popeye Songs.* #UAS672.

1969 United Artists. *Mrs. Portnoy's Retort, A Mother Strikes Back.* #658. This record is perhaps the best known of all Mae's vinyl record performances and is still for sale on many sites.

1974 Mark56 Records. *Betty Boop Scandals of 1974.* MR-602.

1981 Merry Records. *Popeye the Sailorman and his Friends.* #7243.

1996 Angel Records. Motion Picture Soundtrack of *The People vs. Larry Flynt.* This is often described as being archival. Mae performed "Happy You and Merry Me."

I was not able to establish an accurate date for the following:

Maypole Records. *Susie.*

Roost Records. Baby Brother/Ting-Alingle-Jingle. #613

Jubilee Records. Romeo and Juliet, Part One and Two. #3526.

Jubilee Records. Dregnet (Dragnet) Part One and Two. #3525.

Decca. Practicing the Piano. #4473.

Decca. The Broken Record. #680B

APPENDIX 9. UNSUBSTANTIATED CREDITS

People with celebrity status often find their names appear in credits given by others, and Mae Questel is no exception. This appendix contains references or credits others have given Mae, but there was not enough evidence to prove their validity. I was unable to prove that she had appeared in or was involved in these productions (at least to my satisfaction). The only source of this information passed away in 1998. "Search bots" used by search engines (Google, Yahoo!, etc.) pick up many of these incorrectly labeled credits and redistribute them indiscriminately; this does not help. I have included an example in this appendix.

I welcome additional information involving items in this appendix, but please, be prepared to cite your reliable/verifiable source. If enough people can substantiate such claims, a revised edition could result. Mae does deserve that.

1. *One Hour with You.* Movie, 1932. This reference turned up from time to time and needed verification. Some have credited Mae as playing an office worker in this movie, but only at one point could she have been involved. At 1 hour, 06 minutes into the movie is a scene involving two women in an office situation. One woman folds a letter and then hands it to the next woman, who places it in an envelope and then stamps it. Neither

woman even closely resembles Mae Questel, nor at any point in the movie do I either hear or see Mae. After watching it for the second time it occurred to me that there may have been a third woman—the woman who typed the letter and then handed it to woman 2. Perhaps a scene was edited out. Her name is not mentioned in the movie credits.

2. *Goodbye Columbus.* Movie, 1969. *The Monroe News Star* (Monroe, LA) published an article on June 11, 1968, that indicated that Mae Questel signed for *Goodbye Columbus*, produced by the son of opera star Jan Peerce. Starring Richard Benjamin, Ali MacGraw, and Jack Klugman, this movie is about a Jewish love affair. No other article was located with this announcement. The movie ran for about 1 hour 42 minutes. I was neither able to see or hear Mae in this picture. There were some areas of the movie that she would have fit into. Perhaps she served as a stand-in or was victim of another deleted/edited scene. Her name is not mentioned in the movie credits.

3. *Felix the Cat: The Movie.* Animated, 1988. This reference turned up from time to time and required verification. A response from the primary character voice from the movie indicated that Mae did not participate in the movie.

4. *Theater Guild on the Air.* 1945, 1949–1953. Radio, ABC with the sponsor U.S. Steel. There are rare references to Mae's supposed participation, but no specifics as to what Mae's contribution may have been. Her name did not turn up in vintage radio logs as even a guest star. If she did participate, it eluded the record-keepers. Fairly comprehensive records exist of not only the stars but guest stars also.

5. *Mr. Bug Goes to Town.* Animated movie, 1941. Produced by Fleischer Studios and released on December 5, 1941, it ran for 78 minutes. This reference turned up from time to time and required verification. Credits indicate that Gwen Williams provided voicing for the female character. Jack Mercer provided voices also. I was not able to hear Mae in this production. Some credits place Margie Hines as providing voices (though un-credited), and after comparing the two in a sound studio, again, the

character does not sound like Mae Questel. I am not 100 percent certain on this one, but her name does not show up in any reliable credits.

6. *Terry and the Pirates.* Radio/TV, 1941–1947. This one was challenging to say the least. I reviewed 164 radio episodes (old-timeradiodownloads.com) and was not able to hear Mae's voice. All reliable credits list the voices of the Dragon Lady as Adelaide Klein, Agnes Moorehead, Mina Reaume, and Marion Sweet. It is possible that Mae performed voices such as a baby or other singular non-credited voice. Although each radio performance ran about fifteen minutes, I listened to about forty-eight hours of this radio program without a positive result. Although not conclusive, for a guest star such as Mae Questel, I would have assumed mention in a credit was warranted.

The television series has seventeen episodes, with Gloria Saunders appearing in thirteen episodes as the Dragon Lady. Mae's name does not appear in any of these credits either.

7. *Where Have You Been Billy Boy?* Play, 1969. *The American National Biography* (*ANB*) mentions this reference in a short biography of Mae Questel. Although I was able to locate two other performers, I was not able to locate the play, location, date, or any other information about it. There appears to have been a 1996 version, but no help there either. I cannot say conclusively, but that was all I was able to locate. The publisher for the *ANB* was unable to assist me. The *ANB* was the only reference to this performance made about Mae Questel.

8. *Molly and Me.* Play, 1948. The play that opened in New York did not include Mae in any of the credits or in surviving playbills. It is possible that she may have been a replacement. I was also able to watch the 1945 movie of the same name, and I neither saw nor heard Mae in the movie.

9. *70 Girls 70.* Musical play. *The Journal News* from Hamilton, Ohio, published an article on March 26, 1971, with the headline "Mae Questel of Old Betty Boop Cartoon Fame Joined the *70 Girls 70* Musical's Cast." The play was set in New York, consisted mainly of parts for senior citizens, and was performed at City

Center, 131 West 55th Street, Manhattan. Although the play seems perfect for Mae Questel (sixty-three at the time), I am unable to locate her name in any credits. I was not able to hear her in the original Broadway cast recording or find her name in the credits. The *New York Times* published an article about the play not performing for long; no mention of Mae there either. It is possible that she may have been a replacement. There are snippets of the performance online, but no one would respond to my inquires about where the related copy came from or if more is available of the recording.

10. *The Gertrude Berg Show*, aka *Mrs. G. goes to College*. There numerous conflicting accounts of Mae's appearance on this show. The consensus is that she appeared on the first show October 4, 1961, titled "The Baby Affair," as Jenny. Some references list her; others do not. At the time I was accumulating information for this book, I was unable to locate a copy of the show to review. If she did appear on the show, I was not able to spot her.

11. *The Tonight Show with Johnny Carson*. Only a few references mention her appearance on *The Tonight Show* with an airdate of November 14, 1962. There are listings of her as a guest with Rudy Vallee. References to *The Tonight Show* archives do not mention her. At the time I was accumulating information for this book, I was unable to locate a video copy of the show. There are collections available but not of this show.

12. *Somerset*. A few rare references mention Mae appeared on this soap opera in a 1975 episode as Miriam Briskin. I was unable to locate her name in any credits. At the time I was accumulating information for this book, I was unable to locate a video copy of the show. This is not to say that she did not appear on the show, but I was not able to locate her.

13. The picture below is an example of the many incorrectly credited leads that I had to follow up. Jack Mercer and Mae Questel supplied voice characterizations for a Noveltoon cartoon *Counter Attack*, not a kung fu movie. This is a listing from Amazon.com. The poster never responded to my inquiry. I found many references to Mae Questel and Jack Mercer with this VHS

cover on the Internet as a result of search bots finding this information and redistributing it as another of Mae Questel's work. I have had to sift through dozens of such leads.

14. *A Man for All Seasons.* (1967). A search engine directed me to this reference. *A Man for all Seasons* is a 1966 British film about Sir Thomas More (1478–1535). Mae's name is included in the credits on the Amazon.com listing for this movie; she is not mentioned anywhere else. In fact, all the names listed as the cast for the movie *A Man for All Seasons* are actually from *A Majority of One*. The seller indicated that was the information supplied him but would not elaborate. Search bots will mislead on this reference also.

15. *True Story.* The *ANB* entry for Mae Questel indicates that this was one of her contributions. The only information I learned about this show is from seven entries in the Library of Congress Sonic collection. Listed as a radio program (Library of Congress records), it aired from December 17, 1937, to unknown month in 1940, on the NBC Red Network from 9:30 p.m. to 10:00 p.m. The

only name mentioned in these records is A. L. Alexander (1906–1967). What little biographical information is available about A. L. Alexander does not mention *True Story*. Only two program descriptions are given in the seven entries: one a dramatization of a story from the Court of Human Relations, and the other is about marriage.

The only other media that uses that exact name is *True Story* magazine, which is still in publication. If Mae was a guest or provided a voice characterization on the radio show, it appears that she would be the only source to know. The *ANB* does not cite a source or was able to assist me with locating the source(s) of its data.

16. *The Warm Peninsula.* A single source (prabook.org) mentions Mae performing in this two-act comedy play in 1966. After reviewing the playbill, her name does not appear as cast or as an understudy. Although the play opened at the Helen Hayes Theatre in New York, there is no mention elsewhere of her performing. I reviewed several other playbills from different periods with the same result. If she performed, it is not mentioned elsewhere.

17. *Martin Kane, Private Eye.* Only a few sources mention this as one of Mae's contributions. *Martin Kane, Private Eye* was an American radio series and television crime series sponsored by United States Tobacco Company. There are conflicting dates for the radio broadcast and how many aired; the Library of Congress was unable to help. There are only a few sound recordings available. The series made it to television from 1949 to 1954 with twenty-eight episodes on the NBC Network. Mae's name was not in the credits. If she performed on the radio program, it may have been for voice characterizations.

18. *Good Day Show.* A single reference to Mae appearing on a television show called *Good Day*. I do not know which, here are some examples: *Good Day L.A.*; *Good Day New York*; *Good Day Chicago* on WFLD; *Good Day Cleveland* on WJW; *Good Day DFW* on KDFW, Dallas-Fort Worth; *Good Day Iowa* on KFXA, Cedar Rapids, Iowa; *Good Day Alabama* on WBRC, Birmingham, Ala-

bama; *Good Day Philadelphia* on WTXF-TV; *Good Day Tampa Bay*, on WTVT; *Good Day Atlanta*, on WAGA; *Colorado Morning News* on FOX31; *Good Day* on KDVR, Denver, Colorado; *Good Day Orlando* on WOFL; *Good Day Charlotte* on WJZY; *Good Day Austin* on KTBC; *Good Day Maine* on WPFO, Portland, Maine; *Good Day Columbus* on WSYX/WTTE, Columbus, Ohio; *Good Day*, a television-news-music package, produced by Frank Gari, used by some *Good Day* programs; *Good Day!*, a morning show on WCVB-TV in Boston, Massachusetts, that ran between 1973 and 1991; and Doug Stephan's *Good Day*, an American syndicated news/talk program. "Good day!" was the phrase used by American broadcaster Paul Harvey to sign off his daily *News and Comment* broadcasts. *Good Day! The Paul Harvey Story*, a biography by Paul J. Batura, was published shortly after Harvey's death in 2009.

There are many other possibilities, but I believe the reader may have the idea. Each in the preceding list is an independent show, and Mae may have made a guest appearance on one. The list does not cover the radio possibilities.

19. *Good Morning America*. 1980. This would have been season 5 that a single reference is made to. I reviewed 258 episodes from that year and was unable to locate Mae in the credits. Season 5 ran from September 3, 1979, to August 29, 1980, season 6 ran from September 1, 1980, to September 4, 1981. This does not mean that she did not make an appearance; I just was not able to locate her name.

BIBLIOGRAPHY

American National Biography. Supplement 2. Oxford, 2005.

Boemer, Marilyn Lawrence. *The Children's Hour: Programs for Children, 1929-1956.* Scarecrow Press, 1989.

Brantley, Ben. *The New York Times Book of Broadway.* St. Martin's Press, New York, 2001.

Cabarge, Leslie. *The Fleischer Story.* Da Capo Press, New York, 1988.

Carlile, John S. *Production and Direction of Radio Programs.* New York, 1939.

Copyright Office, the Library of Congress. *Catalog of Copyright Entries.* This is a multi-volume series.

Dunning, John. *On The Air, The Encyclopedia of Old-Time Radio.* Oxford University Press, 1998.

Firth, Major Ivan. *The Gateway to Radio.* New York, 1934.

Fischer, Stuart. Kids' TV, The First 25 Years. Facts on File Publications, NY. 1983.

Fleischer, Richard. *Out of the Inkwell. Max Fleischer and the Animation Revolution.* The University Press of Kentucky, 2005.

Godfrey, Donald and Frederic Leigh. *Historical Dictionary of American Radio.* Greenwood Press. Westport, CT. 1998.

Gonzalez, Evelyn Diaz. *The Bronx.* Columbia University Press, New York, 2004.

Guide to the Records of the New York City Board of Education. Compiled by: David M. Ment, Municipal Archives, New York City Department of Records, 2008

Hickerson, Jay. *The New, Revised Ultimate History of Network Radio Programming.* Presto Print, CT, 1996.

Hischak, Thomas, S. *Broadway Plays and Musicals.* McFarland & Co, Inc, Jefferson North Carolina, 2009.

Kanfer, Stefan. *Serious Business-The Art of Commerce of Animation in America from Betty Boop to Toy Story.* Da Capo Press, New York, 1997.

Kilmer, David. *The Animated Film Collector's Guide.* John Libbey and Co. Australia, 1997.

Kurtz, Bill. *The Encyclopedia of Arcade Video Games.* Schiffer, 2004.

Lane, Stewart F. *Jews on Broadway. A Historical Survey of Performers, Playwrights, Composers, Lyricists and Producers.* McFarland & Co, Inc, Jefferson NC, 2011.

Lawson, Tim. Persons, Alisa. *The Magic Behind the Voices.* University Press of Mississippi/Jackson. 2004.

Louvish, Simon. *Mae West. It Ain't No Sin.* Thomas Dunne Books, New York. 2005.

Lynch, James M. *Second Annual Industrial Directory of New York State-1913.* New York State Department of Labor, 1913.

Rivers, Joan. The Life and Hard Times of Heidi Abromowitz. New York, 1984.

Terrace, Vincent. Radio's Golden Years: The Encyclopedia of Radio Programs, 1930-1960. Tantivy Press, 1981.

Wakeman, John. *World Film Directors,* two volumes. New York, 1988.

Webb, Graham. *The Animated Film Encyclopedia.* McFarland & Co., Jefferson, 2000.

Williams, John. *First Annual Industrial Directory of New York State-1912.* New York State Department of Labor, 1912.

Willis, Edgar E. Writing Television and Radio Programs. New York, 1967.

Websites:
Caution should be given to these citations as they are dynamic and constantly changing.
Bettyboop.com (Of course, there is a website for Betty Boop!)
Federal Communications Commission (FCC) http//www.fcc.gov.
Fleischer Studios. www.fleischerstudios.com.
Internet Movie Database. *www.imdb.com/*
Jerry Haendiges Vintage Radio Logs. *www.otrsite.com/radiolog/*
Old Time Radio Catalog. https://www.otrcat.com/. Many old radio shows are now in public domain and can be heard here.

Old Time Radio Downloads. *https://archive.org/details/oldtimeradio*. *Many old radio shows are now in public domain and can be heard here.*

Playbill Vault. *http://www.playbillvault.com*. A wonderful collection of original play bills.

TV.com

TVdays.com-great website for old (1950-1960) commercials.

Printed in the United States
By Bookmasters